PAINTCRAFTS

PAINTCRAFTS

50 Extraordinary Gifts and Projects, Step by Step

Gillian Souter

CROWN TRADE PAPERBACKS

New York

Published by Crown Trade Paperbacks, 201 East 50th Street, New York,
New York 10022. Member of the Crown Publishing Group.

Random House, Inc. New York, Toronto, London, Sydney, Auckland

CROWN TRADE PAPBERBACKS and colophon are trademarks of
Crown Publishers, Inc.

Originally published in Australia by Off the Shelf Publishing in 1996.

Printed in Hong Kong

LIBRARY OF CONGRESS CATALOGING-IN-PUBLICATION DATA
is available upon request.

ISBN 0-609-80035-3

10 9 8 7 6 5 4 3 2 1

First American Edition

Foreword

Mention the word "paint" and some people will conjure up images of stern portraits, vast landscapes, and still lifes. Others will think of large expanses of bare living room wall and a great deal of hard work. Some, however, will happily dream of a few colors on an improvized palette, a couple of brushes, and a great deal of enjoyment to be had. This book encourages you to explore that middle ground of painting which is not overly ambitious and certainly not boring.

Paint can be applied to all kinds of surfaces – wood, glass, ceramics, paper – and each of these requires a slightly different approach. There are also some basic techniques to be discovered: sponging, ragging, spattering, and so on. These may sound simplistic but that is their beauty and they can be the foundation for achieving stunning and sophisticated effects. These various surfaces and techniques are each explored chapter by chapter and each is accompanied by three sample projects:

A personal item, ideal as a gift

Something useful for the home

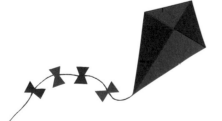

A toy or game for the young

Many of these will make ideal presents and so this book also includes ideas for giftwrap and greeting cards. Of course, you may find that you can't bear to part with the finished project, in which case there's only one solution – make two of everything!

Contents

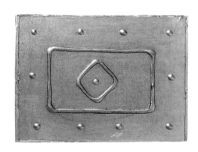

Paints

The basic ingredient in paint is pigment: finely ground particles of color. These are mixed with a binding material, and it is the nature of the binding substance which dictates how the paint behaves.

Gouache and poster colors are opaque water-based paints; the latter is less expensive and is ideal for children. Acrylic paints, which are also water-based, contain a plastic binding medium which is flexible and quick drying. Some give matte finishes, others dry like a gloss enamel. Most are available in a wide range of ready-mixed colors.

Watercolor paints contain very fine pigment and a gum binder. They produce a translucent wash and so are shown to best effect on white paper.

Marbling inks and silk paints are two types of liquid color with specific uses.

Oil paints, made with a mixture of pigment and vegetable oil, must be handled quite differently: they are thinned and cleaned up with turpentine or mineral spirit and dry slowly. They do, however, offer a richness of color and texture.

The binding medium in each paint type determines how it behaves on certain surfaces: watercolors will not adhere to china; poster paints crack on flexible fabrics. Surface-specific paints are available but they tend to be relatively expensive so another option is to combine paint with a formulated liquid or medium. For more information, see page 12. If children are involved, make sure the paints and mediums used are non-toxic.

If you plan to try lots of paint projects, it's worth investing in the basic colors in a variety of paint types. This lets you work on different surfaces and achieve varying effects, and you can always mix extra colors.

Acrylic paints are perhaps the most useful type for anyone doing craftwork.

Poster paints can be bought as a powder, as blocks, or ready-mixed.

Some fabric paints come with nozzles for application direct from the tube.

Watercolor paints can be bought in tubes, as blocks, or even as pencils. The pencils are especially easy to use as you can color a design and then apply water with a brush. All the patterns in this book have been colored with such pencils.

Oil paints are generally expensive and less easy to work with. They are recommended for only a few of the projects in this book.

Some paints are formulated to adhere to smooth surfaces such as glass and china. Most of them can be heat-fixed in a domestic oven for a durable finish.

Equipment

Paint can be applied with all sorts of utensils, most commonly a brush. Brushes come in different shapes and fibers and it is important to choose the appropriate one for the project. Flat brushes are suitable for covering large areas, round ones for painting lines or shaped strokes. Tips also vary: flat brushes cut at an angle are useful for precise work; a pointed liner brush is necessary for fine details.

Brushes can be soft, made from nylon or animal hairs, or have stiff bristles, as with stencil brushes or "fitches" which are good for spatter work. Experiment with brushes to see what strokes they make. After painting, wash all brushes in soapy water and store them with heads upright.

Paint can also be applied with a sponge, a toothbrush, a rag, or any number of household items. You can also raid the kitchen cupboards for a palette on which to mix paint: old saucers or the lids of plastic cartons are ideal. Other equipment may be needed to prepare surfaces, transfer patterns, or to cut and fix materials.

Equipment and materials for each project are listed in a box above the main picture. When the list includes "painting equipment" you will need a container of solvent (water or turpentine, according to the paint), suitable brushes, and plenty of newspaper to cover your work area.

Left: equipment for transferring designs.

Film containers are perfect for storing small amounts of acrylic paint.

Sandpaper and wet-and-dry paper are required for the preparation and completion of many projects.

Cotton swabs are handy for cleaning up small mistakes.

The sponge brush is an ingenious tool for applying a glaze smoothly.

Below are a basecoating brush, two flat brushes, a round brush and a fine liner. Select a brush of a suitable size and shape for the particular task in hand.

Masking tape is useful for holding tracings or stencils in place and, of course, for masking off non-paint areas.

Basic Techniques

There is no need to be tentative about the application of paint. It can be rolled, splashed or spattered onto a surface. It can then be scraped, smudged, or wiped. None of these techniques demands any great skill. A little more confidence is required when painting designs freehand, but this will come quickly when you start working with brushes.

As the projects in this book involve a range of surfaces, various techniques are required to cut and shape those surfaces. Anything unusual that you need to know is discussed in the opening pages of each chapter and it is worthwhile reading through that text before undertaking the relevant projects. These projects offer a starting point and will hopefully encourage you to explore techniques which catch your interest.

Using Paint Mediums

A medium is a liquid that is added to pigment in order to change its properties. Various commercial mediums are available to alter a paint's consistency, gloss, flexibility, or its adherence to a surface.

To thicken paint, choose from white glue, non-fungicidal wallpaper paste, or a commercial medium. By adding one or other of these to acrylic paint, you can create an opaque or transparent glaze that spreads easily and dries more slowly, allowing you to work with the paint longer.

Extender or retarder medium is a paint additive that slows down the drying time without thickening it, an aid when painting false marble and other such finishes.

Textile medium makes an acrylic paint flexible when dry, while glass-and-tile medium allows acrylic paint to adhere to a smooth surface. Both can be heat-fixed for greater durability. As dedicated fabric or ceramic paints can be expensive, such untinted mediums can be a good investment.

When buying a medium, read the label carefully. Make sure that it can be mixed with the type of paint that you plan to use. Check too whether the finish it will create – gloss, satin, or matte – is what you desire.

Preparing Surfaces

While it may be tempting to just jump in and start splashing the paint about, the project will be a better one if you prepare the surface properly. If you are rejuvenating old furniture or objects, any old paint should be stripped off or sanded back until the surface is smooth. A dark color may need to be concealed with a white undercoat; gesso is ideal for this.

Fabrics are often treated with a size or coating after they have been manufactured and if you plan to apply paint or dye, you will need to wash the fabric thoroughly first. Use plain soap and, if possible, allow the fabric to soak in soapy water for an hour or so before rinsing it and then hanging it up to dry. At this point, you might staystitch the edges to prevent the fabric from fraying. Finally, press it smooth with an iron.

If working with new wood, you may need to fill holes with a commercial wood filler. Sand any rough areas or edges with medium-grade sandpaper. A coat of sealer or water-based varnish may also be applied to give the paint a better ground.

Terracotta is a very porous surface. An application of sealer or water-based varnish will prevent it from soaking up too much paint and will also make the item a bit more water-tight.

Wash glass and china objects thoroughly and rinse them in a solution of vinegar and hot water to remove any greasy marks. Dry the object thoroughly before painting.

Old metal objects may need to be treated with rust converter. A coat of a rust-inhibiting primer before painting will prevent future rust problems.

Transferring Patterns

To transfer a pattern for a project, lay transparent kitchen paper or thicker tracing paper on the book and trace over the lines with a soft pencil. If the patterns are reversible (as many of them are) simply turn the tracing over, place it on the surface to be painted and run the pencil over the lines. If it is not reversible, you can run a pencil over the reverse and then redraw over the first face, or you can place transfer paper under your tracing.

Mark fabric with tailor's chalk, a dissolvable marker or a soft lead pencil. It may be necessary to tape the pattern and fabric to a window and trace the lines. Alternatively, cut out the traced pattern and use it as a paper template.

Scaling or resizing a pattern is easy to do if you have access to a photocopying machine. If you don't, you can use the method described below. If the instructions in a project say to enlarge a pattern by 200%, you will need to double its size. 300% would be three times the size of the original printed pattern, and so on.

To enlarge a pattern by hand, use the squaring up method. Trace the pattern and rule a ½ " grid over it. If the instructions specify to enlarge it by 200%, rule a 1 " grid on a fresh piece of tracing paper and copy the pattern square by square.

Mixing Colors

Most makes of paint are sold in a wide range of colors, which is wonderful if you require a large amount of French blue or burnt sienna. For those occasions, though, when you just need a touch of purple or dab of orange, it is easier and far less expensive to mix your own colors.

For a basic set of paints, you will need blue, yellow, red, black and white. For the greatest range of potential colors, you should buy three blues: cerulean, Prussian and ultramarine (or cobalt); a cool lemon yellow and a warm yellow; an orange-red and a cooler red, plus black and white.

When mixing colors, start with small quantities or you can find yourself with far too much of an unusual color. Pastel shades are colors mixed with white.

When combining colors in a design, consider this wheel of primary and secondary colors. Complementary colors—those opposite one another—result in bold contrast. Adjacent pairs create a more muted, harmonious effect. Pairs of alternate colors, such as blue and yellow, can be striking. Including white in a design tends to boost other colors.

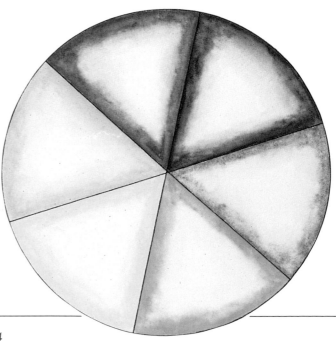

Painting Tips

Working with paint is a matter of confidence and this will grow with every project you attempt. The most important thing is to enjoy what you're doing.

Before starting, get a glass of water for diluting paints and rinsing brushes. It's a good idea to work in a room which has a sink, so you can refresh this regularly and wash up easily afterwards.

You may not need to transfer all the details of a pattern; some key marks may be sufficient. Before painting a design freehand, practice the brushstrokes on scrap paper.

The consistency of the paint is important: thin paint may run in some situations, thick paint may not be suitable for fine detail. You may need to add a medium (see page 12) for extra transparency or to thicken paint.

You can avoid visible brushstrokes by applying paint with a sponge or a sponge brush. A fingertip can also be a useful painting tool. Wipe off mistakes with a damp cotton swab, or paint over them with the basecoat color.

Finishing Touches

Beautiful paintwork deserves to be well-protected and can even be enhanced by special treatment in the final stages.

There are various ways to give new paintwork the appearance of age. For some of these techniques, refer to pages 144-5.

A coat of varnish protects the paintwork and can make the colors appear richer. You have a choice between a water-based product and a polyurethane one. The latter offers a lovely rich finish, but also tends to cast a yellow tinge, especially over time. Before varnishing, remove all dust from the article. Use a soft flat brush and apply the varnish in long strokes in the one direction. For a high gloss finish or for added protection, apply further coats, sanding lightly between coats and leaving the article to dry each time in dust-free conditions.

Furniture wax can be applied to wooden articles after varnishing, giving a gentle sheen and extra protection. A touch of gold wax can produce an especially elegant finish.

Remember to fix fabric and ceramic paints so that the finished items can be used and washed. Fabric paint is usually fixed with an iron and ceramic paint in an oven but you should read the instructions on the paint container for specific details of temperature and time.

Paper

Paper is not the most stable material on which to paint: some papers can buckle with too much moisture. It is, however, a relatively inexpensive and readily available material, and so it is a good one for children to use exuberantly, or for adults to start with. Moreover, once you have understood its limitations, the opportunities for paper and paint will be many and varied.

Before you choose a paper for painting, it is worthwhile considering the nature of the material. Paper is a sheet of intertwined fibers which is pressed flat. It can be pressed smooth or with a rough pattern. When it is formed, paper has a matte surface and is quite absorbent. Paper intended for writing is usually coated with a size which prevents inks and paints from seeping in. Unsized paper will be more suitable in most cases.

The heavier the paper, the more suitable it is for use with water-based paints. Watercolor paper is the best option, but drawing paper, or "cartridge paper" as it's also known, can be used for most paintwork. Very heavy card or board is less flexible but can also carry heavier paints as a result. As a general guide, use watercolors on paper, and poster paints, gouache, or acrylics on board or on papier-mâché.

There are countless uses for paper and paint. We tend to think of paper as a two-dimensional material, limiting projects to framed pictures or wrapping paper. Papier-mâché removes this boundary, making all kinds of shapes and structures possible. Paper can also be pleated, cut, rolled, or used for covering solid objects such as lampshades, books, or boxes.

A retractable craft knife and a cutting mat are necessary for most paper projects; a bone folder can be useful.

Papier-mâché
*Strips or scraps of torn newspaper
can be pasted around a base or a
mold to form a solid but lightweight
object. The paste also acts as a
sealer, so any paint can be applied
to papier-mâché projects.*

Tinted photographs
*Dip a matte black-and-white
photograph in diluted bleach
until the black tones fade. Rinse
it well and dry it. Paint with
watercolors, building up areas
of strong color by applying
a second coat when dry.*

*Introduce an extra
degree of creativity into
the craft of découpage,
by painting your own
prints for cutting and
decorating.*

PROJECT 1

Badges

Papier-mâché is a fun and inexpensive technique for making decorative pieces. These bright badges would be perfect prizes at a children's party.

YOU WILL NEED
cardboard
newspaper
a pencil
scissors
paste
water-based paints
water-based varnish
painting equipment
safety pins
felt

1 ◄ Draw the outline of the shapes onto packing cardboard with a pencil. Cut out each shape with strong scissors or a sharp knife. Make up a small amount of wallpaper paste, or mix up flour and water to the consistency of white glue.

2 ◄ Tear some narrow strips of newspaper. Dip each strip in the paste and remove the excess paste with your fingers. Apply the strips onto the cardboard bases, overlapping them and smoothing each one down. Cover each base with several layers of newspaper and then leave to dry. Paint white.

3 ► When the white basecoat is dry, draw the designs onto the badges. Apply paint, allowing each tint to dry before applying the next. Add the gold details with a fine liner brush. When the paint is dry, apply a coat of water-based varnish.

4 ► Cut a piece of felt to match each badge. Cut two small slits in the felt, open a safety pin and weave it through the slits. Glue the felt onto the back of a badge, so that the safety pin is secured but can be opened and closed.

PROJECT 2

Paper Fan

YOU WILL NEED

watercolor paper
watercolor paints
a sponge
a ruler
a pencil
a knife & mat
embroidery threads
painting equipment

This project offers a gentle introduction to working with watercolors. Such a fan can serve as an unusual decoration or as a useful accessory on a summer's evening.

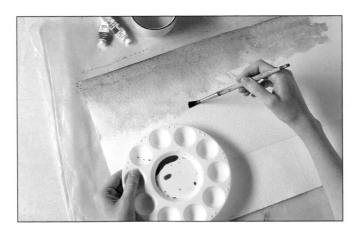

1 Cut a piece of watercolor paper approximately 10½ " wide and 43 " long; you may need to cut two pieces and join them later. Moisten the paper with a damp sponge. Paint a color wash along the top of the paper, thinning the paint as you work inward. Paint a reversed band of color along the base.

2 On a sheet of paper, measure and mark a series of lines 1 " apart. Using these as guidelines, run a bone folder or the back of a knife over the watercolor paper, scoring lines from top to bottom.

3 Fold along each of the scored lines, turning the paper over each time, to create a concertina. Smooth along each fold with the bone folder or the back of your fingernail to press the crease.

4 If necessary, glue the two folded sections together so that the joint is concealed. Near the base of the fan, pierce a hole with a sharp implement. Thread a piece of strong thread through the hole and bind the base of the fan tightly.

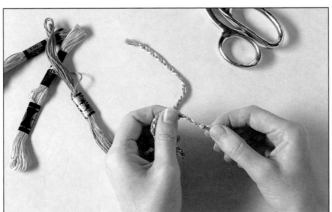

5 Cut 30 " lengths of embroidery threads in three different colors. Knot the ends together and secure this knot to a stable object. Braid by twisting one side strand over the central one, then the other side strand over the central one, and so on. Knot the end and tie the cord to the fan binding.

PROJECT 3

Découpage Bin

Give an old wastepaper bin a second life with some hand-tinted découpage. The classical prints can be photocopied from this book, or you might find others you prefer elsewhere.

1 ▶ *See page 13 for details on preparing old metal for painting. Mask the base and rim with tape and spray a cream basecoat. Apply a second coat if necessary. Photocopy the drawings on page 156, calculating how many you need to fit around your bin.*

2 ▶ *Paint the photocopied prints with watercolors. Do not use too much water as photocopying paper is not very absorbent. You need not be too careful about painting within the outside lines as the designs will be cut out. When dry, apply a coat of fixative or thinned white glue to seal the colors.*

3 ▶ *With a pair of curved scissors, cut around the outside lines of the design. This is easy for the square shapes but the border design will require more care. Arrange the border sections around the bin and glue each one in place with a generous amount of white glue. The last section may need to be modified to fit.*

4 ▶ *Arrange the square designs around the bin and glue them in place. Glue down any edges of paper that are lifting. Varnish the bin, allowing it to dry between each coat. The more coats you apply, the better the general effect.*

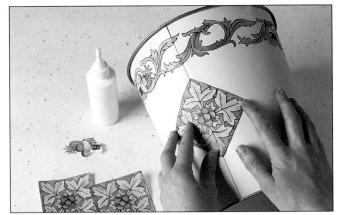

Wood

Some timber has a beautiful grain and you should avoid the temptation to cover it up with an opaque paint. Consider applying an earth-coloured glaze or a solution of white paint and sealer that gives a chalky appearance but is thin enough to show off the grain. Acrylic paint, on the other hand, is good for disguising cheap timber or manufactured woods such as chipboard, ply, and fiberboard.

Raw timber should be sanded lightly once any holes and imperfections have been filled with a commercial wood filler. Some wood can absorb large amounts of paint. Sealing it first with a commercial sealer or a water-based varnish provides a foundation for the paintwork.

Old furniture is a painter's delight, whether it be your own or salvaged from a junk shop. Look out for pieces that are well-made and have an interesting shape but are in need of attention. You will need a smooth surface for painting so remove any old paint which is cracked or peeling by softening it with paint stripper and then using a paint scraper. Fill, sand, and seal, as for new wood.

You do not need a great deal of expensive equipment to make your own projects from wood. A handsaw and fretsaw are needed for cutting and shaping timber. Transfer patterns onto wood with tracing paper or colored transfer paper. You will also need plenty of sandpaper, in various grades of coarseness, for preparing and finishing projects as paint-work on wood is particularly suitable for distressing (see pages 144-5).

Wooden toys are a wonderful thing in this age of synthetics and they give you an opportunity to paint bright colors and bold designs. There are plenty of small and useful articles for the house – a letter holder, a mug rack, placemats – that are easy to make and offer you surfaces for a range of painting techniques and styles.

When working with wood, a few basic tools are necessary for cutting and shaping projects.

Dowel rods are easy to cut and can be used in various simple projects.

The wooden shapes on the left have been cut with an electric jigsaw. A variety of such pre-cut shapes, along with old-fashioned wooden clothes pegs such as those on the right, are available from some craft stores.

Picture dominoes
Cut a length of flat timber into pieces twice the width. Sand each piece and cut a groove in the middle. Basecoat them, then draw and paint a series of motifs. Outline the pictures and the groove in black.

PROJECT 4

Napkin Rings

Dowel offers lots of possibilities when colored with inks or paint. You could make a matching candle ring, or a picture frame covered with dowel pieces.

YOU WILL NEED
thin dowel
a cardboard tube
a saw & knife
a ruler & pencil
colored inks
painting equipment
glue
sandpaper
skewers
elastic bands

1 Mark a strong cardboard tube into 1½ " sections with a pencil. Use a sharp craft knife to cut the cardboard rings neatly.

2 Mark a length of thin dowel into 2 " sections and cut these with a handsaw. Sand the ends of each piece smooth. Check that you have enough pieces by holding them around the cardboard ring.

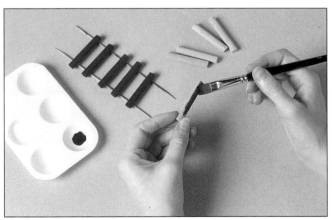

3 Color half of the dowel sections with one color of ink, and the other half with a contrasting color. This process can be messy; work over scrap paper and leave the sections to dry on two parallel skewers.

4 Apply strong glue to the outside of the cardboard ring and position the dowels, alternating the colors. Hold the pieces in place with an elastic band until the glue has set. For extra decoration, bind some gold thread around each napkin ring.

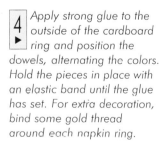

PROJECT 5

Kitchen Rack

If you have some wall space and need extra storage, this easy-to-make project is a neat solution. For a hat rack, space the hooks further apart on a longer backboard.

1 ▶ *From a length of timber 3½" wide and ¾" thick, measure and cut a piece 19" long. Sand the edges smooth. Undercoat it white and allow to dry. Brush on a colored topcoat and, while it is still wet, wipe it with a sponge. Allow to dry.*

2 ◀ *Apply masking tape around the perimeter of the board so that ¼" is covered. At each end, apply another piece of tape to reveal a ¼" strip of painted timber. Paint this in a contrasting color.*

3 ▶ *When dry, remove the tape at the ends and apply a long strip at top and base to create a complete border trim. Paint this in the contrasting color and allow to dry before removing all the tape. Apply a coat of water-based varnish.*

4 ◀ *Position the hooks along the board and mark through the screw holes with a sharp pencil. Drill a small hole at these points and then screw the hooks in place.*

PROJECT 6

Bookends

A rainbow adds a splash of color to a child's room and these bookends may even help to keep some degree of order amid the chaos!

YOU WILL NEED

timber
a handsaw & fretsaw
sandpaper
a ruler & pencil
a compass
glue
a drill
nails & screws
water-based paints
gloss varnish
painting equipment

1 On a length of 3½ x ¾" timber, mark and cut two pieces 8" long and two more, each 5¾" long. Sand edges, rounding the corners on one end of each piece.

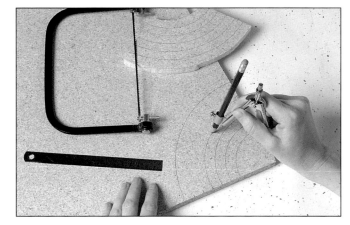

2 Drill a hole in the center of each short section. Apply glue to the base of a short section and position this on the long section to form an "L." Secure this with three nails, hammered in from the back of the long section.

3 You will need chipboard ½" thick. At a corner, mark 2" in from each edge, then make six more marks at ½" intervals. Fix a compass to a 2" radius, place the point at the corner, and join the first two marks with an arc. Adjust the compass to the next mark and continue on, joining each pair of dots to mark out a rainbow. Repeat on another corner.

4 Cut along the first and last lines with a fretsaw or jigsaw. Sand the edges of the rainbow. Paint the arcs in six rainbow colors.

5 Glue each rainbow in place on an L-bar. Screw through the base to fix. Varnish each bookend with gloss varnish.

Fabric

Many possibilities are opened up when you choose fabric as a surface for painting. Textiles share some of the properties of other fibrous materials, but are stronger than paper and more flexible than wood.

Select fabrics made from natural fibers, such as cotton, linen, or silk, as these will absorb paint better than synthetics. Choose fabric of a suitable weight, flexibility, and durability for the intented use: what is ideal for the guestroom may not suit the playroom.

Fabrics are often treated with a size or dressing after thay have been manufactured and this affects their ability to absorb and hold paint. Wash new fabric thoroughly in soapy water, then rinse and dry it well. Iron new and old fabrics well to remove any creases which might spoil your paintwork.

To transfer a design onto fabric, tape the cloth onto a window over a tracing and mark over the lines with tailor's chalk, a pencil, or a dissolvable marker. Alternatively, cut out the tracing and use it as a template.

A wide array of paints formulated for use on fabrics can be found in most craft stores. These include paints with a pearl or metalic sheen and some which puff up when heat is applied. Most are sold in small tubes with handy nozzles for direct application, but they are relatively expensive. Instead, it may be worth investing in a bottle of textile medium which can be added to acrylic paints, making them flexible and permanent.

Fabric paints must usually be heat-fixed so that they are color-fast and so the item can be washed repeatedly. This is often done by ironing the wrong side of the painted fabric, or ironing with a piece of paper between paint and iron. The instructions provided by the manufacturer will usually specify a temperature and setting time.

All sorts of useful projects for the home can be made with decorated fabric, including curtains, tablecloths, bedcovers, and cushions. Clothing, either bought or homemade, can be turned into unique and personal items. Soft toys are always popular and the addition of a few painted details will make them all the more special.

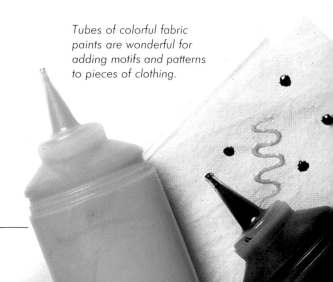

Tubes of colorful fabric paints are wonderful for adding motifs and patterns to pieces of clothing.

Jar covers
Preserves made for gifts or for a fair are even more appealing when they're beautifully packaged. If you're bottling a lot of one type, it's worthwhile cutting a stencil to represent that fruit. Instructions for stenciling are on pages 120-1.

Silk painting
Special liquid paints in strong colors are available for painting on silk. These flow freely through the fibers of the silk and so may need to be contained with an outliner such as gutta. Clear gutta can be washed out after painting, but metalic gutta becomes a feature of the design, as in these small designs.

PROJECT 7

Jugglers

These charming beetles can be used as juggling balls or simply as small companions. To draw the markings, you will need a tube of fabric paint with a fine nozzle.

YOU WILL NEED

red cotton fabric
tracing paper
a pencil
fabric paint
scissors
sewing equipment
beans or seeds
black cord
glue

1 ▶ Trace the main lines of the pattern below and lay the tracing on red cotton fabric. Mark around the tracing with a pencil, allowing a ¼ " seam. Draw the wings, eyes and spots with a tube of black fabric paint.

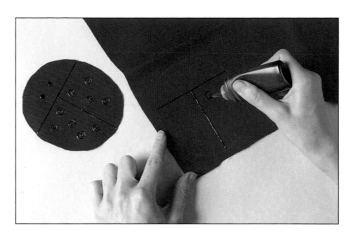

2 ▶ When the paint is dry, cut out the decorated top section and a plain section the same size for the base. Lay the two together, right sides facing. Cut a piece of black cord and knot it at one end, then dip both ends in glue to prevent fraying. Make another feeler and position the two between the fabric pieces, as shown.

3 ▲ Sew a seam around the edges of the layered pieces, leaving a gap at one edge for turning. For greater durability, zigzag the edges to prevent fraying. Turn the beetle inside out and fill it almost full with seeds, grains or beans. Handsew the opening closed.

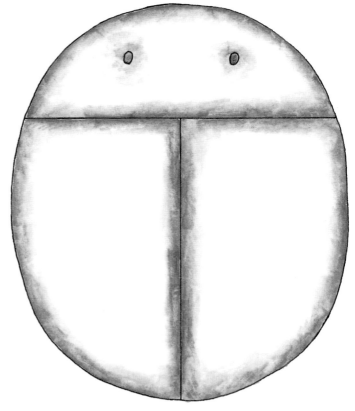

PROJECT 8

Floor Mat

YOU WILL NEED

artist's canvas
a ruler
a pencil
acrylic paints
fabric medium
varnish
painting equipment
fabric tape

Painted mats made from strong cloth were popular during the 18th century. This one is painted in the hues of the Arab world but can be adapted to suit a particular room.

1 ▲ Cut a piece of canvas measuring 42 x 30 ". Fold a 1 " hem all around. Measure and mark a 2 " border. Divide the design area into six 12 " squares and transfer the pattern below into each square.

2 ▲ Mix acrylic paint with textile medium according to the manufacturer's instructions or use commercial fabric paints. Paint the base colors with a flat brush.

3 ▶ Outline all shapes with a fine liner brush in dark cinnamon paint. When dry, apply several coats of varnish. Turn the mat over and tape the hem down with fabric tape.

PROJECT 9

Silk Scarf

YOU WILL NEED
thin white silk
outliner
a frame
pins
a pencil
a ruler
silk paints
painting equipment

The most difficult part of making this beautiful scarf is transferring the design. After that, it's a simple act of coloring in!

1 ▲ Roll and stitch a hem around a square of silk. Mark a border around the edge. Enlarge the pattern below to fit a quarter of the marked panel and transfer the design onto the silk, quarter by quarter (see page 14).

2 ▲ Make a frame by cutting a square, slightly smaller than the silk, in a sheet of cardboard. Pin the silk over the square, so that the fabric is taut. Apply gold outliner along the lines of the design, using a plastic bottle and a large nib. Make sure that all the intersecting lines connect or paint will escape through the gaps. Let the outliner dry.

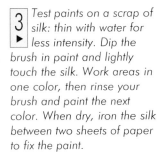

3 ▶ Test paints on a scrap of silk: thin with water for less intensity. Dip the brush in paint and lightly touch the silk. Work areas in one color, then rinse your brush and paint the next color. When dry, iron the silk between two sheets of paper to fix the paint.

China

Applying color to glazed ceramics was once the preserve of those who had access to a kiln. These days, there are paints that can be used on china and fixed in a domestic oven, and there are others that can be simply left to dry on this surface. This chapter suggests some of the ways these paints can be used to decorate plain white china.

Most of the white china available will be crockery designed for holding food. However, ceramic paints aren't food-safe and you must not paint areas which will come in contact with food or mouths. Pieces which will only have a decorative function can be completely painted, but such items as mugs should have unpainted rims.

A range of paint options are available for china painting. Water-based ceramic paints are available in an array of colors and are made permanent

Chinagraph pencils will mark designs easily on china. Cotton swabs are useful for removing painting mistakes.

by fixing them in a kitchen oven. Solvent-based paints are known as "cold ceramic paints" because they are not heat-fixed; they are also less durable and should only be used on decorative pieces. Alternatively, a medium can be added to acrylic paint, allowing it to adhere to glazed china. This can be less expensive in the long term and the mixed paints can be heat-fixed.

Brushstrokes tend to show up clearly on china. This can be part of the appeal, or you can avoid them by using a sponge to apply the paint. Ceramic paints should not be thinned with too much water. Tape and adhesive stickers are useful for masking areas from the paint.

Follow the instructions on the paint containers for the method of heat-fixing, as too much time or heat in the oven can discolor the paint. Cold ceramic paints, which should not be heat-fixed, can be coated with a varnish (usually sold with the paint range) which protects the paintwork.

Teapot tile
Mark a design on a white tile with a chinagraph pencil. Paint the base colors and outline them in black with a fine liner. Mediterranean colors are ideal for this project.

Molded patterns
Platters and bowls with bas-relief designs of fruit or flowers can be tinted with ceramic paint to accentuate the shapes.

PROJECT 10

Tick-Tack-Toe

Tick-tack-toe is played by two people taking turns
to place a token on the grid. The first to place three
in a row wins that game.

1 ◄ With a chinagraph pencil or other marker, mark a border around the edge of a large white tile. Divide the tile into nine squares, with even bands dividing them. Cut squares of adhesive plastic and position them so that the squares are masked.

Note: White, glazed tiles are inexpensive and are usually available in various sizes. Alternatively, you can paint tinted tiles with a basecoat of white before decorating them.

2 ► Using a sponge, apply paint over the unmasked areas of the tile to create a border and a grid of lines.

3 ► On five small tiles, mark a circle with a pencil and compass (or draw around a round object). On four more tiles, mark an "x." Paint over these with a fine liner.

4 ► Cut a sheet of felt in pieces to match each of the tiles. Glue a piece onto the back of each tile with white glue.

PROJECT 11

Potpourri Bowl

Here is a pretty design to start you painting freehand on china. If you make a mistake, it's a simple matter to wipe away the error and correct it.

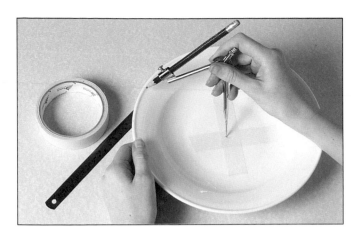

1 Lay two strips of tape across the center of the bowl. Measure from edge to edge and mark the center with an "x." Use a compass to mark two rings around the rim: the distance between them may depend on the shape of the bowl but should roughly match the pattern.

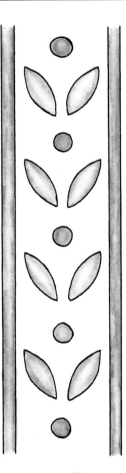

2 Paint over the two circles using a medium paint brush. First paint the outer circle, let this dry, and then paint the inner circle.

3 Between the circles, mark a dot at regular intervals. If you find the last one does not fit neatly, adjust the position of those around it. Paint over the dots.

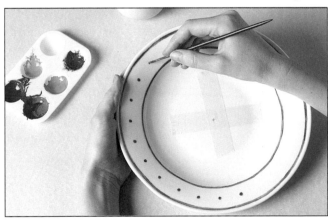

4 Paint a pair of leaves between each of the dots. When the paint is dry, set it in an oven as per the manufacturer's instructions.

PROJECT 12

Teapot

YOU WILL NEED
a white glazed teapot
a marker
self-sticking dots
ceramic paints
painting equipment

If bright colors and modern design are your cup of tea,
then this is the pot for you! For even greater effect, make
a matching set of cups and saucers.

1 ◀ Using a chinagraph pencil or other marker, draw lines around the rim, spout and handle of the teapot.

2 ▶ Stick adhesive dots randomly around the body of the teapot. With a flat brush, paint short strokes at right-angles, creating a cross-hatched effect. Apply paint up to the marked lines.

3 ▶ Once the paint is dry, carefully remove the paper dots. Paint contrasting spots of paint, not quite filling the area left by the sticker.

4 ▶ With a fine liner brush, paint a black four-sided shape with curved sides. Paint a matching figure over it to create an eight-pointed sun. When the paint is dry, set it in an oven as per the manufacturer's instructions.

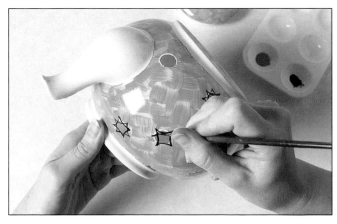

Clay

In this chapter, we turn our attention to unglazed ceramics. This can include earthenware, terracotta, and objects modeled from craft clay, all of which remain porous and so tend to absorb paint. Accordingly, they need to be treated in a different way to glazed china, the subject of the last chapter.

For aspiring potters without a kiln, air-hardening craft clay is a wonderful material. Items made with it will not be waterproof but it is ideal for small projects such as beads, a teapot stand, or the houses in Project 15. Those who don't wish to get clay under their fingernails may like to apply their brushes to terracotta items instead. Garden centers sell a range of pots, planters, and plaques which are relatively inexpensive and which can be personalized with paint.

Unglazed ceramics can be decorated with several types of paint, including solvent-based cold ceramic paints and acrylics. Lime wash, a solution based on lime, produces a lovely chalky effect on terracotta as you can see in Project 14.

Before painting a design on a pot, cut a collar of paper to fit around it and plan out your design. A soft pencil is ideal for marking a design on unglazed ceramics. If you need to wash an old pot clean, make sure it is quite dry before you apply paint; the exception is lime washing, when you should dampen the pot first.

Painting directly onto untreated terracotta can give an uneven finish which is often very attractive. For more even paintwork, apply an undercoat of clear sealer. This will make the ceramic less porous and so easier to work on.

Apply a thin coat of white emulsion onto terracotta and wipe it off again while still wet. The result is a softened, aged appearance.

Wall plaque
Molded terracotta shapes
painted with bright colors
make eye-catching pieces.
The background has been
sponged and the detail of
the fish has been picked out
with a dark color.

Bright beads
Roll a piece of clay and cut it into
even sections, then roll each into
a ball. Pierce each with a skewer and
allow to dry. Paint the beads with
acrylics and apply a coat of varnish.
String them on a doubled length of
strong thread.

Potted presents
As well as large garden pots, you
can paint miniature terracotta pots
from craft stores. Fill them with
dried flowers or bath salts as a
gift, though make sure you seal
the inside in the latter case.

PROJECT 13

Buttons

Clay is fun to model and can be used for many everyday objects. These buttons, however, are decorative and could not be washed with a garment.

YOU WILL NEED
air-hardening clay
a rolling pin
a coin
a sharp knife
a ring
a skewer
acrylic paints
water-based varnish
painting equipment

1 ▶ Roll out a lump of clay to a thin sheet; a piece of plastic over the clay will prevent it sticking to a rolling pin. Place a coin of a suitable size on the sheet and cut around it with a sharp knife. Cut as many buttons as you require.

2 ◀ Smooth the edges of each piece with a moistened finger. Press a ring or the flat end of a marker pen to create a depression in the center.

3 ▶ Pierce two or four holes in the center of each button with a skewer. Leave the buttons to dry.

4 ▶ Paint the buttons with a white basecoat of acrylic paint. With a fine brush, add stripes of color radiating out from the depression and paint the center. Once the paint is dry, apply a coat of water-based varnish.

PROJECT 14

Terracotta Pots

YOU WILL NEED
lime wash
white acrylic paint
a pencil
tracing paper
masking tape
painting equipment

Inexpensive terracotta pots can be given an air of classical antiquity with a coat of lime wash and the touch of a brush.

1 ▶ Prepare the surface by moistening the pot with a sponge. Apply a coat of lime wash, a pigment based on lime. Allow it to dry.

2 ▶ Trace the pattern in pencil onto a strip of tracing paper. Turn it over and pencil over the lines of the design.

3 ▶ Transfer the design onto the pot rim, holding the tracing in place with masking tape. You may need to adjust the design where the start and finish meet.

4 ▶ Using a fine liner brush, paint the design with white acrylic paint. Note that the paintwork on these pots is not weatherproof so they should be protected from the weather. A coat of sealer on the inside of the pots will make them suitable as flower pots.

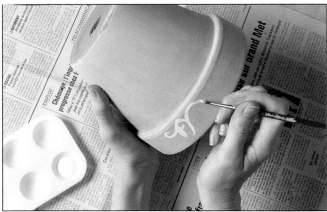

PROJECT 15

Dutch Houses

YOU WILL NEED
air-hardening clay
wire
a pencil
acrylic paints
water-based varnish
painting equipment

These charming pieces are modeled on the canal houses in Amsterdam, but they will delight children from any part of the world.

1 ◄ Work clay into a block by throwing it down onto a flat surface on one face or another. Continue until one face of the block measures 1½ x 3 ". Holding a piece of thin wire taut, cut two corners off the block to shape the roof of the houses.

2 ◄ Slice the block into even sections no thicker than 1 ". Make sure each house stands straight upright. Smooth the edges with a moistened finger. Leave the houses to dry on an old newspaper; this may take several days.

3 ◄ Basecoat each house in a different color of acrylic paint, applying a second coat when ready. Trace the house shape onto scrap paper and plan the arrangement of windows and other details.

4 ◄ Use a very fine liner brush to paint the detail in white acrylic paint. Don't forget to paint the sides and back, if you like. Apply a coat of water-based varnish.

Glass

Glass tends to be overlooked as a craft material, but it offers plenty of possibilities for the painter. Old jars can be turned into attractive vases; sheets of glass can become works of art to hang in a window. If you are lucky enough to have access to a kiln, you can use paints formulated for firing to decorate functional glassware which can be used in contact with food, and washed repeatedly. The rest of us must restrict ourselves to ornamental pieces which can be washed gently on occasion.

For children who wish to paint on glass or acetate, add some white glue to poster paints; this is inexpensive and easy to wash up. For adults, the same options are available as for china painting (see the earlier chapter). A commercial medium can be added to acrylics, helping them to adhere to glass and allowing them to be heat-fixed in a domestic oven. Water-based ceramic paints and solvent-based cold ceramic paints are also available in a wide range of colors.

Solvent-based glass paints have a consistency much like nail polish and tend to flow. They can be contained within an outliner sold with the range of paints. If you choose lead-colored outliner, the effect can be remarkably similar to stained glass. The paintwork can be given some protection with a special varnish.

When heat-fixing water-based paints on glass, follow the instructions on the bottle carefully. Always place painted glass in a cold oven and do not remove it until it has cooled.

Etching cream can be applied over masked glass like a paint; the unmasked area will lose its polished finish.

Gold outliner for cold ceramic paints can be quite pleasing on its own. It can be applied direct from the tube.

Glass art
Drip different colors of paint into a bottle or vase and turn it slowly until the paint dries.

Unfired paints won't survive repeated wushing so you would usually only paint decorative pieces. However, you might consider painting glass-ware for a special meal or occasion.

PROJECT 16

Scent Bottles

Make your own floral water by simmering fresh petals, paint a few heart motifs on an ordinary bottle, attach a colorful tag, and you have a charming gift.

YOU WILL NEED
glass bottles
cold ceramic paints
gold outliner
turpentine
a brush
flower petals
a saucepan
a strainer
acetate
gold thread

1 ▶ Collect old bottles with an attractive shape—such as olive oil bottles—and wash them in a solution of hot water and vinegar. Draw the heart motif with a tube of gold-colored outliner. Make sure the scrolls at the top of the heart join, to contain the filling color.

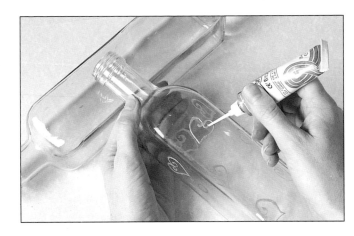

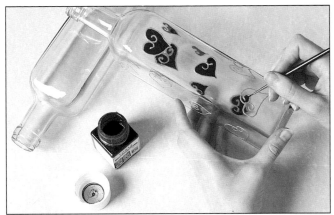

2 ◀ When the outliner has set, fill in the hearts with cold ceramic paint in the color of your choice. The paint will spread once it has been laid on the glass, so you will not need to brush too close to the outlines.

3 ◀ To make floral water, place 8 tablespoons of scented fresh petals in a saucepan and cover them with 3 cups of water. Cover the saucepan and simmer for 30 minutes. Remove from the heat and, when the mixture has cooled, strain it through a fine mesh or a piece of cloth.

4 ▶ Fill the bottles with floral water. Make tags by repeating the painting process on pieces of acetate. When the paint is dry, cut the acetate around the outline, pierce a hole at the top and tie a tag around the neck of each bottle.

PROJECT 17

Etched Vase

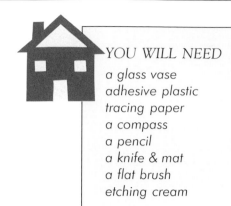

YOU WILL NEED
a glass vase
adhesive plastic
tracing paper
a compass
a pencil
a knife & mat
a flat brush
etching cream

Etching cream makes it possible to decorate glass in a very subtle way. The delicate motif on this vase is a Chinese character which bears the meaning "Spring."

1 ◄ Cut a sheet of adhesive plastic large enough to cover one side of the vase. In the center, use a compass to draw a circle with a 2 " radius. Cut this circle out with a sharp knife and stick the remaining piece onto the vase.

2 ▲ Transfer the pattern onto the circular cutout, either by tracing directly onto the plastic, or by using tracing paper (see page 14). Cut along the lines with a knife and stick the pieces onto the vase in the center of the circle.

3 ► Make sure the adhesive lies smoothly on the glass by running a thumbnail over the edges. Apply the etching cream onto the bare glass as per the instructions on the bottle. The cream should be applied thickly with smooth strokes, using a flat brush or a sponge brush.

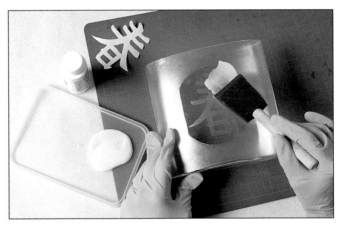

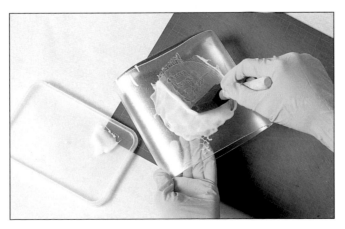

4 ◄ Leave the cream on the vase for the recommended time, then rinse it off with water. Peel the adhesive stencil off the vase.

PROJECT 18

Picture Pane

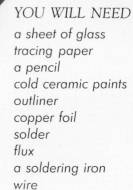

Cold ceramic paints can create the effect of stained glass when used with a black outliner. Make an instant aquarium to hang in the window of a child's room.

YOU WILL NEED
a sheet of glass
tracing paper
a pencil
cold ceramic paints
outliner
copper foil
solder
flux
a soldering iron
wire

1 ▶ Trace the fish pattern on page 157. With a glass cutter, cut a sheet of glass the same size as your pattern or have a piece cut at a glass store. Lay the glass on the tracing and draw over the lines with a tube of lead-colored outliner.

2 ◀ When the outliner has set, fill in the design with cold ceramic paints. The paint will spread once it has been laid on the glass, so you will not need to brush too close to the outlines.

3 ▶ Wrap a strip of copper foil around the edge of the glass. Copper foil, flux and solder can be bought from leadlighting stores. Twist two short pieces of wire to form hanging loops.

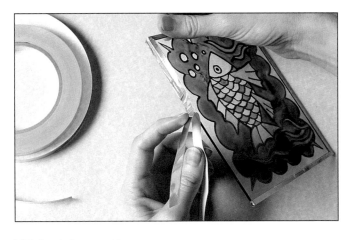

4 ◀ Brush flux onto the copper strip. Lay the hanging loops at the top of the sides and brush with flux. Heat the soldering iron and melt solder all over the copper foil, securing the loops at the same time. Turn the panel over and solder the other side. Secure a wire or ribbon to hang the pane.

Rag & Sponge

Large, unbroken areas of paint can be a little tedious on the eye and are easily softened with the use of a rag or sponge. Which item you choose and how you use it determines the effect: this chapter includes ways of applying paint to a fresh surface and ways of removing it once paint has been laid down.

In each of these, whatever is beneath the paint will be revealed, so you may wish to paint a complementary base color. Usually, this is paler than the topcoat: either white or a paler shade of the feature color.

Ragging is a subtractive process: a glaze is applied to a surface with smooth brushstrokes and then worked on while still wet. While the technique is loosely called "ragging," you can use any scrunched-up material from paper, to fabric, to a scrap of plastic kitchen wrap: each will produce a different effect. Make sure the material is clean and lint-free.

This material can then be rolled over the surface of the glaze, or it can be dabbed onto it. Ragging tends to be dramatic, breaking up the glaze with definite markings.

Stippling is akin to ragging: the wet painted surface is dabbed lightly with a dry synthetic sponge to create a subtle pattern. Both techniques must be worked quickly before the glaze dries, so do not attempt too large an area at a time.

Sponging on paint is more straightforward, partly because drying time is not a factor. Different types of sponges can be used: a marine sponge will create larger patterns than a household sponge. Dampen the sponge so it is springy and load it with paint. Test by dabbing onto scrap paper: if the result is muddy, sponge the excess onto the scrap paper before dabbing the sponge haphazardly over the work surface. Once dry, a second color can be sponged on if you want a mottled effect.

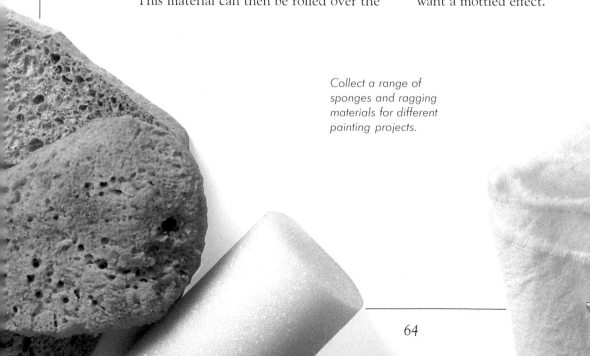

Collect a range of sponges and ragging materials for different painting projects.

Rag & sponge effects

Right: ragging, using a piece of crumpled paper.

Bottom right: stippling with a fine synthetic sponge.

Below: sponging with a household sponge.

Applying paint with a sponge allows you to control the amount of color, to the point of graduating colors from a solid hue to almost nothing.

PROJECT 19

Shape Cards

YOU WILL NEED
stiff cardboard
a pencil
a ruler
a knife & mat
water-based paints
a sponge

Make a color-and-shape matching game for young children by sponging paint onto cards through a set of templates. Keep the colors bright and make sure the paint is non-toxic.

1 ▶ Load a sponge with non-toxic paint and apply paint all over one side of a sheet of white cardboard. Turn the sponge as you work so the paintwork is irregular.

2 ▶ Cut the cardboard into 2½ " squares, using a sharp knife and a ruler. For a complete set, you will need 32 cards.

3 ▶ Cut four squares of thin cardboard, each 2½ " square. On each of these, draw a different shape: a circle, a square, a triangle and a cross. Cut the shape out with a knife, leaving you with a stencil.

4 ▶ Lay a stencil on the white side of a card and lightly sponge paint through the shape. Make two sets of each combination: green circles, green crosses, red circles, and so on, so you have matching pairs.

PROJECT 20

Cannisters

Spongeware gives a kitchen a French provincial air and this treatment is a wonderful way to rejuvenate old and rusted tins.

YOU WILL NEED

airtight food tins
rust converter
rust primer
water-based paints
water-based varnish
a sponge
painting equipment

1 Apply rust converter to the rusted areas of old tins and their lids, following the product instructions. Then apply a coat of rust-inhibiting primer to the entire surface.

2 Basecoat the outside of the tin white, applying a second or third coat if necessary. If the lid is a tight-fitting one, do not paint around the rim as it may make it difficult to open and close later.

3 Load a damp (not quite moist) sponge with cobalt blue paint and dab the excess onto scrap paper. Sponge lightly around the tin, reloading the sponge with paint as required.

4 Paint blue onto the rims of the base and lid with a fine liner brish. When the paint is dry, apply a coat of water-based varnish for protection.

PROJECT 21

Coffee Mugs

YOU WILL NEED
white glazed mugs
ceramic paints
masking tape
a lint-free cloth
painting equipment

Ragging the topcoat produces a fiery effect here. When painting mugs or cups for use, make sure you leave the rim free of any paint.

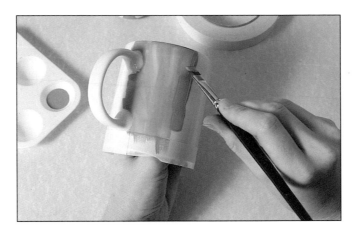

1 ◄ Mask the rim of each mug with a wide piece of masking tape. Apply a basecoat of orange-yellow ceramic paint with a flat brush using long, smooth strokes.

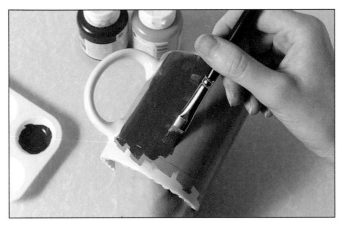

2 ◄ Apply a topcoat of orange-red with long, smooth brushstrokes. Work quickly and move onto the next step before starting another mug.

3 ► While the topcoat is still wet, press a lint-free rag (or a piece of plastic wrap) against the paint. Twist the rag so that the pattern is not regular as you work around the mug.

4 ► With a fine liner brush, paint rust-colored lines beneath the rim and on the handle of each mug. When dry, heat-fix the painted mugs by following the manufacturer's instructions.

Scratch & Scrape

Precise brushstrokes are not the only way to achieve detail in paintwork. Removing paint from a surface in a pattern or design is another way of adding interest to an item.

All kinds of household objects can be commandeered for these projects. An old wide-toothed comb is ideal, but for scraping wider marks, you may need to cut your own combs from stiff cardboard. Anything with a sharp point will do for scratching paintwork.

It is important that the surface for decorating is not too porous, or it will absorb paint which cannot then be removed. A basecoat of white paint or sealer will avoid this problem. The frame in Project 30 is based on a similar process of isolating the topcoat and could as easily be included in this chapter.

When combing or scraping a pattern, you must work quickly while the paint is wet.

A glaze, a mixture of paint and a water-based medium, has an extended drying time and so is more suitable than plain paint. Do not make it too thin or it will flow back into the combed marks. Apply it to the surface thickly with a large flat brush, or with a flat sponge brush.

Combed patterns can be long and flowing or regulated and precise. Combs with wider teeth tend to create a more primitive effect than, say, the more sophisticated combing in Project 24. More complexity can be introduced by using combs of different widths, intersecting each other at right angles to create the effect of woven fabric. A narrow piece of card (effectively a single "tooth") can be used like a broad-nibbed pen to scrape calligraphy letters and shapes in a glaze.

Scratching paint with a sharp implement gives you more freedom to create detailed figures but these will also be less bold. Geometric shapes or simple motifs are most easily identified, or you could try using the scratching tool like a pencil and "sketching" pictures with scratched lines. Be careful not to tear the surface material, especially if it is paper.

A compass point, a stylus, the end of a brush, a knitting needle: all are potential tools for scratching designs.

Foil-covered board is available in various metalic colors. Drawing ink or acrylic paint can be painted onto it and, when dry, scraped off to form interesting patterns.

Scratching and scraping are ideal ways of turning plain sheets of paper into attractive giftwrap. Use strong paper which can bear a thick paint glaze.

PROJECT 22

Serving Tray

*The basketweave pattern on this sturdy tray gives it
a strong country flavor. The technique is quite simple
and quick to work.*

1 ▶ Prepare the surface of an old tray (see page 13) or buy a plain wooden tray. Basecoat the tray with several coats of white acrylic paint. When the basecoat is quite dry, lay masking tape along the edges of the inside panel.

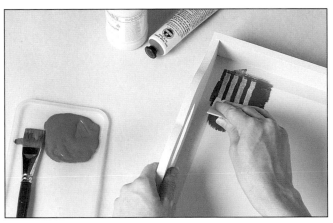

2 ▲ Measure the area to be decorated and cut a piece of card that will divide into it. Snip darts into one end of the card to make a simple comb.

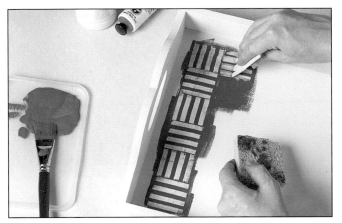

3 ▲ Tint glaze medium with a water-based paint (see page 12). Lay glaze within the masked panel and comb a stroke which covers a square area.

4 ▶ Comb at a right angle to the first stroke. Continue working across the panel, applying glaze and then combing. The size of area that you work should depend on how quickly the glaze dries.

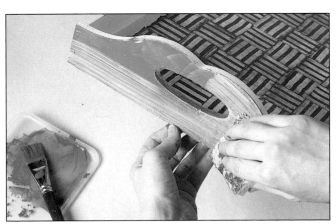

5 ◀ Apply a coat of glaze to the sides of the tray and, while the paint is still wet, wipe each surface with a dry sponge. When the glaze has dried, remove the masking tape and varnish the whole tray.

PROJECT 23

Tree Baubles

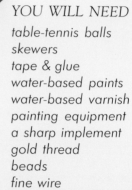

These bright, naive decorations have been made with table-tennis balls but polystyrene or papier-mâché ones would also work well.

1 ◀ Pierce a ball with a skewer and basecoat it white. Dry between coats using a polystyrene stand, or by weighting the skewer over the edge of a table. Bind the middle of the ball with a thin strip of removable tape. Paint the top and base in one color, using the skewer to turn the ball while working.

2 ◀ Remove the tape and paint a band of contrasting color. With a fine liner brush, paint a thin line on either side of the band.

3 ▶ With a sharp implement, scratch a series of intersecting lines over the top and base. Scratch stars at regular intervals around the band. Outline the band and add extra detail between it and the thin lines. Dust off any particles and apply a coat of water-based varnish.

4 ▶ Twist a small piece of wire to form a loop and thread a bead over the ends. Push both ends into the skewer hole and glue to secure. Tie a hanging loop of gold thread or ribbon through the wire loop.

PROJECT 24

Portfolio

The combination of wavy and straight lines creates the illusion of watered silk, which is shown off to best advantage on a large project, such as this folder.

1 ◀ Tint a glaze medium (see page 12) with a water-based paint. Cut two identical large sheets of strong paper. On the first, lay the glaze with a sponge or flat brush. With a broad-toothed comb, mark a series of wavy lines across the paper.

2 ▲ While the glaze is still wet, comb straight lines across the paper. Once the sheet is complete, glaze and comb the second sheet and leave them both to dry.

3 ▲ Cut two pieces of cardboard and cover each one with a sheet of combed paper, gluing down the flaps on the back. Tape two corners of each board with bookbinding tape as shown.

4 ▶ Lay the boards patterned side up with a slight gap between the bottom edges. Use tape to join the two boards along this spine. Open up the joined boards and mark the width of your ribbon on the inside top. Cut matching slits in both sections.

5 ▶ Thread a piece of ribbon through each slit and secure it on the inside of each board. Cut a large piece of thin card, slightly narrower than the portfolio's width and twice its height. Score two lines to match the spine width and glue the lining in the portfolio.

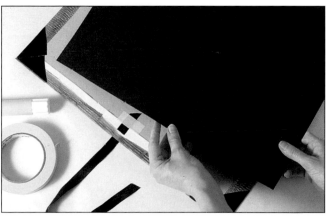

Spattering

This method of applying paint has great child-appeal, possibly because it can be extremely messy. It is also an excellent way to apply paint sparingly in a subtle manner. While it stands on its own merit as a finish, it can also be combined with other paint techniques to achieve various false finishes, as in Projects 27 and 50.

Until you master your toothbrush, you will need to cover your work area with plenty of newspaper. It is a good idea to set your work in a large cardboard box so that the sides of the box act as a shield. It is wise to restrict yourself to water-based paints when spattering, and to wear old clothes.

The consistency of the paint is very important as paint which is too thin will drip and paint which is too thick will blob. Test it by spattering onto scrap paper and adjust the paint if necessary.

For a fine spatter, load an old toothbrush, stencil brush, or nailbrush with paint and run your finger or a knife over the bristles towards you so that a spray of paint is sent in the opposite direction. You can control the result by moving closer to or further away from your work.

For a bolder effect, use a brush with longer bristles, such as one designed for basecoating. Once loaded with paint, this can be tapped on the stick of another brush held over the work area. Alternatively, if you're feeling very expressive, try flicking the brush at the surface, throwing heavy spatters of paint onto it. The paint will need to be the consistency of milk for this to work.

Applying several colors in a fine spatter can be very effective, as some pointillist painters have demonstrated. Allow each color to dry before applying the next so that each color remains distinctive. Try spattering light colors on a dark background and vice versa. By masking different areas at different stages, you can create quite a complex design with an essentially simple technique.

A toothbrush gives a fine spatter; a large, coarse brush produces larger spots. A spray can creates a fine mist of paint.

Spattering

Use natural objects and pieces of cut card to mask off areas from the paint. For a sharp outline, they must lie quite flat against the surface.

Paperweights
Basecoat river-smooth pebbles with paint and spatter them with a contrasting color. Personalize them with a monogram.

81

PROJECT 25

Umbrella

YOU WILL NEED
an umbrella
tracing paper
a pencil
a knife & mat
adhesive plastic
fabric paint
a toothbrush
an iron

Spatter over a mask to create this Celtic motif. As the paint and fabrics used will vary, the umbrella may not remain waterproof, but it will always make a lovely sunshade!

1 ▲ Trace over the pattern and transfer it onto the back of clear adhesive plastic (see page 14). Cut along the lines with a sharp knife, removing the motif in one piece.

2 ▶ Carefully peel the motif from the backing paper and position it on a panel of the umbrella. Smooth the edges down with your fingers. Load an old toothbrush with some thin fabric paint and run your finger over the bristles (test this first on scrap paper). Finely spatter over the motif.

3 ◀ When the paint is dry to the touch, remove the mask and work on another panel. When the umbrella is complete, allow the paint to dry thoroughly, then fix it according to the manufacturer's instructions.

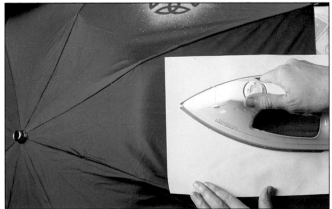

PROJECT 26

Magic Wand

Flecks of gold or silver paint add a touch of magic and mystery. Here they can turn a piece of plywood into a handy wand for a fairy or wizard.

YOU WILL NEED

plywood
dowel
tracing paper
a pencil
a saw & sandpaper
strong glue
a toothbrush
water-based paints
water-based varnish
painting equipment

1 ◀ Trace the pattern and transfer it onto plywood, enlarging it if desired (see page 14). Cut out the star shape with a fretsaw. Cut a length of dowel for the handle. Sand the star's edges and the ends of the dowel.

2 ◀ Glue one end of the dowel onto the star with strong adhesive. Paint the wand a rich blue, applying two coats if necessary.

3 ▲ With your fingertip, wipe gold paint around the edges of the star and along the handle. Load gold paint onto an old toothbrush and run your finger over the bristles to spatter finely onto the star. When dry, apply a coat of water-based varnish.

PROJECT 27

Porphyry Coasters

YOU WILL NEED
wooden coasters
acrylic paints
glaze medium
a sponge
painting equipment
a toothbrush
water-based varnish

*Porphyry is a rock once highly valued by the Romans.
Here, a combination of spattering and stippling techniques
is used to mimic the rich hues of purple porphyry.*

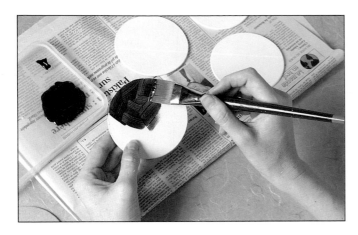

1 Basecoat the coasters white. When dry, apply a dark purple glaze (see page 12) with a flat brush.

2 While the glaze is still wet, press it lightly with a dry synthetic sponge, creating a textured effect known as stippling. Allow this to dry.

3 Dilute some white paint to a milky consistency. Load a large brush with this and spatter it by tapping the brush on another brush. Test this on scrap paper before working on the coasters; you want to achieve medium-sized dots of paint.

4 Load an old toothbrush with gold paint and run your finger over the bristles to spatter finely onto the coasters. Allow to dry.

5 Carefully paint the edges of each coaster with gold paint. Varnish the coasters, waiting for one side to dry before varnishing the other side.

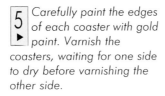

Resistworks

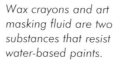

Certain waterproof substances do not sit well with water-based pigments and this antipathy can be put to good use. In some ways, resistworks are like stenciling or using masking tape, but because the resisting substance can often be applied in a controlled manner, you have greater flexibility of design.

Art masking fluid, available from art supply stores, is possibly the most flexible of all. This fluid, which contains latex, is usually used by watercolor artists. It must be shaken well before use and then applied with a wet brush. After a few minutes, a color wash can be painted over it. When this in turn is dry, the masking fluid is removed with a soft eraser, or by rubbing it with your fingertips.

Melted wax is ideal for working resist designs on fabric, although children should be supervised when working with hot wax.

It can be applied to the fabric with a brush or a piece of thick card. The fabric is then dyed and the wax is later removed by melting it with an iron. By applying wax to different areas and using different colored dyes, the batik artist can create an image with some depth and complexity. For a much simpler project, use a white candle as a pencil and draw a design on paper, then paint a color wash over it.

Wax crayons can be used in the same way as the candle and offer the added benefit of color. When covered with a thick coat of black acrylic or poster paint, which can then be scraped off, the colors of wax crayons are set off beautifully, as in Project 30.

White glue drawings, applied directly from a container with a nozzle, are fun to make and can be surprisingly artistic. Work on thick paper and when the glue has set, color it with inks or watercolors.

Wax crayons and art masking fluid are two substances that resist water-based paints.

Batik giftwrap
In batik work, patterns are made with melted wax, preventing the dye from permeating the material on those areas.

Dyed eggs
Dab some vegetable oil onto an egg which has been blown (see page 99) and attach a fresh leaf. Tie the egg in a section of old stocking and immerse it in food dye until stained.

Glue painting
Draw a design in white glue and, once it has set, paint over it with a color wash for a subtle but pleasing result.

PROJECT 28

Gift Bags

Gift bags are an ideal means of wrapping awkwardly-shaped presents. These are patterned with art masking fluid which resists the watercolor wash.

YOU WILL NEED
brown paper
masking fluid
watercolor paints
painting equipment
a pencil
a ruler
a knife & mat
glue
a holepunch
cord or ribbon

1 ▶ Shake the art masking fluid well. Brush the fluid onto brown paper in a pattern of your own choosing. Don't allow the fluid to dry on the brush; remove it with water.

2 ▶ When the masking fluid has dried, paint a wash of watercolor over the paper. When the paper is dry, remove the masking fluid by rubbing it with your finger or with a soft eraser.

3 ▶ On the paper, mark out a basic giftbag shape to the desired size; the pattern for this is on page 157. Cut it out and fold along the dashed lines. Glue the side flap and then glue the base flaps, folding in the end flaps first.

4 ▶ Press the sides together gently to form a side pleat. Use a holepunch to make two sets of holes at the top the bag. Cut two lengths of ribbon or cord. Thread each through two holes and knot the ends inside the bag to form two handles.

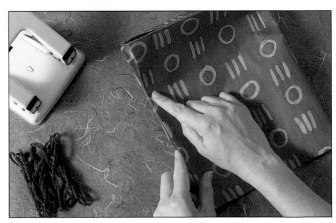

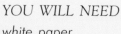

PROJECT 29

Doorplate

*Mark the domain of a child's bedroom with a smart
doorplate. The writing in this one is formed by using
candle wax to resist paint.*

YOU WILL NEED
white paper
cardboard
string
white glue
a pencil
a knife & mat
a ruler
a candle
water-based paint
painting equipment

92

1 ▶ On a piece of cardboard, sketch out the child's name. Dip string in white glue and arrange it along the lines of the letters on the card. Allow the glue to dry.

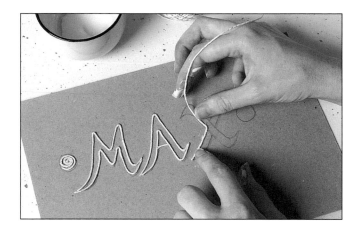

2 ◀ Place a sheet of white paper over the string letters. Rub over each of the letters with the base of a white candle. Make sure the paper does not slip while you work.

3 ◀ Use a flat brush to apply a wash of water-based paint over the paper. The letters should remain white. Leave the paper to dry.

4 ▶ Cut a piece of cardboard larger than the name and glue the painted paper onto it. Cut the corners, turn the flaps over and glue them down at the back. Cut a frame from black card and glue it over the name. Glue a piece of ribbon on the back for hanging the doorplate.

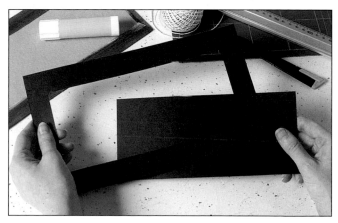

PROJECT 30

Picture Frame

Black paint sets off the vibrancy of wax crayons
very well. When making this project, choose tones
to suit the photograph you plan to frame.

1 Measure the photograph or picture you wish to frame. On a piece of white cardboard, mark up a suitable size of frame and cut it out with a craft knife. Cut a backing section the same size, but without a window. Color the frame with wax crayons.

2 Apply a thick coat of black water-based paint, such as acrylic or poster paint. Let it dry.

3 With the end of the brush or some other implement, scratch a design around the frame. You may wish to plot this out first on scrap paper. Apply a coat of water-based varnish.

4 Secure the photograph between the frame and the backing section. Trace the pattern for the stand onto cardboard then cut along the solid lines. Run a knife lightly along the dashed lines and bend them. Glue the flap of the stand onto the backing.

Marbling

What accounts for the timeless appeal of marbling as a means of decorating paper, fabric, and the like? Maybe it's the endless detail and complexity of the swirls and patterns and the subtle color effects. Or perhaps it's the fact that each marbled piece is unique, that no intricate design can be perfectly reproduced. Or maybe it's the seemingly magical transfer of color and pattern, one minute floating on water, the next fixed permanently on a solid surface.

The technique of marbling (not to be confused with the false finish) is based on the fact that certain inks or paints will float on water rather than mix with it. By laying paper or fabric onto the surface of a water-based bath, the paint can be transferred and fixed.

Three-dimensional objects can also be marbled by lowering them into the bath, as in Project 31.

The type of colors and the size (used in this context to mean water thickened with an agent) can vary. The thicker the size, the greater the control you have over the patterning of the colors. When marbling inks are floated on unsized water, as in Project 32, a pretty, swirling pattern is all that can be obtained.

Project 33 demonstrates what can be achieved by floating oil paints on a size of water thickened with wallpaper paste. The paint can now be manipulated with skewers or combs to create identifiable, if somewhat coarse, marbling patterns.

The greatest control is achieved by floating watercolor paints on a carrageen size. This is also the most complicated method of marbling, requiring lengthy preparation and an array of materials and is well covered in more specialized books.

Droplets of paint can be lowered gently onto the surface of the size with an eyedropper or drinking straw.

Marbling inks, available in sets, can be floated on water. The colors are subtle rather than strong. Here, they have been transferred onto fabric, which was then made into a pouch.

Oil paints can be thinned with white spirit or turpentine and floated on water. Student's oil paints work better than the more expensive types.

◄ Prepare the size and allow it to rest in a deep tray. Spatter the thinned paints onto the surface and then use a skewer or comb to create a pattern. Lay the paper or fabric onto the size so no air bubbles are trapped and then lift off the marbled work. Skim off any remaining paint with strips of newspaper and repeat the process.

A classic piece of marbling, made by floating watercolors on a carrageen size and then combing it in a specific sequence. All kinds of beautiful things can be created with marbling, either on paper or fabric.

Using a size of thin wallpaper paste, oil paints can be manipulated into patterns which hold their position long enough to capture them on paper or fabric.

PROJECT 31

Marbled Eggs

YOU WILL NEED
hen eggs
alum
acrylic paints
wallpaper paste
a pin
a skewer
straws
wire
varnish

Most people think of marbling as a technique to decorate paper or fabric, but three-dimensional objects can also be enhanced in this way – including the humble egg.

1 ▶ *Eggs should be at room temperature. Pierce a hole in the top and base with a pin and enlarge these with a skewer. Poke the skewer well into the egg to break the yolk. Blow hard into the top hole and collect the contents in a bowl. Rinse the egg by submerging it in water, then let it drain well.*

2 ▶ *Thread thin wire through the egg and loop it at either end to secure the egg. Dissolve a teaspoon of alum in 2 cups of water. Submerge the egg in the alum solution and then leave it to dry. The alum will encourage paint to adhere to the surface.*

3 ▶ *Mix a size from non-toxic wallpaper paste and water. The consistency should be that of egg white. Pour it into a bowl and let the solution stand for an hour. Add a little water to acrylic paints to thin them. Use straws to scatter droplets of paint onto the size.*

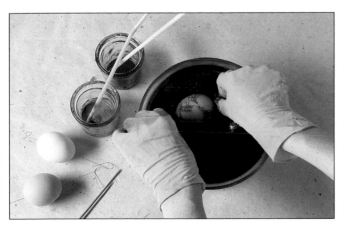

4 ◀ *Swirl the paint gently with a skewer and lower the egg into the size, submerging it. Lift it out vertically and hang it to dry by the wire loop: do not rinse off the size. Once the paint is dry, apply a coat of varnish and hang it to dry again. Remove the wire and arrange eggs in a bowl.*

PROJECT 32

Heart Mobile

Marbling inks produce a soft effect, ideal for this nursery mobile. If you add lavender to the filler, a soothing scent will be released as the mobile twirls.

YOU WILL NEED
silk or cotton fabric
a deep tray
marbling inks
a skewer
a pencil & paper
scissors
fiber filler
sewing equipment
ribbon
a wooden hoop

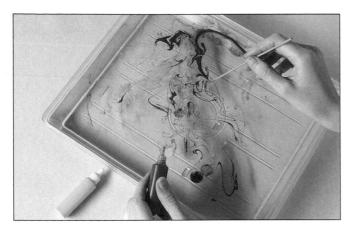

1 Prewash and press the fabric. Fill a deep tray with water. Float marbling inks on the surface and swirl the inks with a skewer. Lay the fabric on the water so no air is trapped beneath. Lift it off and lay it flat to dry.

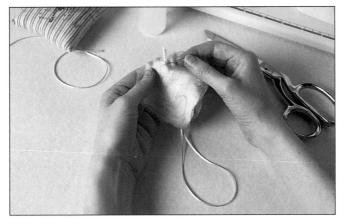

2 Trace the pattern onto paper and cut out a template. Use this to cut shapes from the marbled fabric, with a 1/4 " seam allowance all around. Cut two sections for each heart. Stay-stitch around the edges or apply a fray-prevention liquid.

3 Lay the two sections together, right sides facing. Cut 18 " of ribbon, fold it in half and sandwich it between the fabric layers so that the ends of the ribbon are aligned with the top edges of the heart shapes. Sew a narrow seam, leaving a small gap for turning. Snip darts at the sharp corners and turn the hearts inside out.

4 Fill the heart with fiber filler. Handsew the opening closed. Paint a wooden hoop white. Loop the hearts onto the hoop and arrange them evenly. Tie four more pieces of ribbon at intervals around the hoop and attach them to a central ring for hanging the mobile.

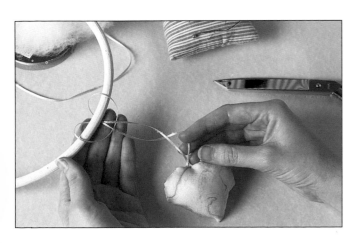

PROJECT 33

Brush Pot

Everyone who works with paint needs a pot to store brushes upright. Making your own also allows you to demonstrate your marbling prowess.

YOU WILL NEED
white paper
wallpaper paste
marbling equipment
oil paints
mineral turpentine
thick cardboard
a cardboard tube
glue
a ruler, knife & mat
water-based varnish

1 ▶ Mix a size from non-toxic wallpaper paste and water. The consistency should be that of egg white. Pour it into a bowl and let the solution stand for an hour. Dilute the oil paints with white spirit or turpentine and scatter droplets onto the size.

2 ▶ Use a skewer or comb to make patterns. Shown here is a nonpareil design, made by raking a series of lines from top to bottom, then across, and then down again. Lay a sheet of paper onto the size. Lift off the paper and wash off any size under a cold tap. Dry flat.

3 ▶ Measure and cut a 4 " length of large cardboard tube (available from stationery shops). Use the tube to mark a disk for the base on thick cardboard. Cut this out and glue it to one end of the tube.

4 ◀ Roll a piece of marbled paper around the tube and glue the edge. Cut darts in each end of the paper, fold them over and glue them down. Cover the base with a disk of marbled paper. Insert another piece inside the tube to conceal the darts. Apply a coat of water-based varnish.

Stamping

Both this chapter and the next are concerned with printing. The simplest way this can be done is by applying paint to an object which is then stamped onto a surface. This object can be cut in a particular shape or, for greater complexity, it can have sections scooped out from the stamping surface, so that parts of it do not print.

Stamps can be fashioned from any material which will hold paint or ink. Porous materials, like foam, are obvious choices but even surfaces which seem smooth, like linoleum, hold paint surprisingly well. The latter has the advantage of being easily carved with purpose-bought tools, allowing extra detail in the design.

When planning your design, keep in mind that the action of stamping will reverse it. This means that if you include lettering or any element with a specific orientation, you must cut the stamp as a mirror image. Fill in the non-printing areas of the design with pen to remind you which

sections to remove. Erasers and potatoes can be cut with a sharp knife: cut down along the outlines of the design and then cut across to remove unwanted sections. If cutting linoleum, warm it slightly first, and keep your hands away from the line of cutting. You will need a straight blade for cutting along the design lines, and a U-gouge and V-gouge for scooping out areas: a set of inexpensive linoleum cutters will include these.

Paint can be applied to the stamp in various ways. Sometimes, it is best to brush it on or apply it with a roller. Foam stamps can be dipped into paint spread on a flat surface. For solid stamps, such as potato-cuts, you can make a stamp pad by pouring thinned paint over a household sponge in a dish.

Stamping is an excellent way to create repeat patterns. A design based on a square or a triangle allows you to produce various patchwork effects by turning the stamp. With some planning, you can stamp a continuous border on a wall or a piece of fabric.

The surfaces of an eraser, cut with a knife, make excellent stamps and are especially suitable for use with ink pads. This one stamp can produce a range of patterns.

Strong, fresh leaves and other natural objects, such as halved apples or oranges, can produce beautiful prints.

A carefully planned design with a corresponding beginning and end allows you to stamp a continuous border pattern. This one, stamped with fabric paint, is based on a Roman motif.

PROJECT 34

Night Light

Stars and moons shine brightly on this stamped lampshade, making it ideal for a bedside table. If you can't buy a blue shade, you can cover an old frame with fabric.

YOU WILL NEED
a lampshade
erasers
gold paint
a knife
tracing paper
adhesive labels
a pencil
masking tape
painting equipment

1 ▶ Draw or trace the designs onto adhesive labels (see page 14 for information on transferring patterns). Cut out each shape and stick it onto an eraser which will be used as a stamp.

2 ▶ With a sharp knife, cut around the adhesive shape. Make partial cuts parallel to the face, removing the non-design areas. Remove the paper shape.

3 ◀ Brush some gold paint onto the stamp and press it firmly onto the lampshade. Work around the shade, alternating stars and moons, and reapplying paint to the stamp each time.

4 ▶ Apply strips of masking tape around the base of the lamp and paint bands of gold for extra decoration.

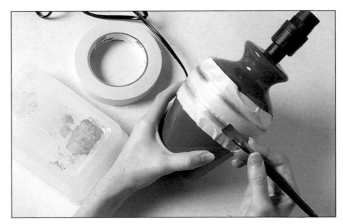

PROJECT 35

Costume Hats

YOU WILL NEED
colored cardboard
scrap paper
a pencil
a knife & mat
potatoes
water-based paints
glue
painting equipment

Children will have great fun making and then wearing these cardboard hats but an adult should help by cutting the potato stamps.

1 Use scrap paper to make a model hat which fits the child's head. The crown is a band with one jagged edge; the pirate hat is a curved piece with long side bands; the medieval one is a triangle with one curved edge. Using the paper template, cut thin cardboard with scissors or a knife.

2 Cut a potato in half to create a flat surface. Lay the potato onto absorbent paper to soak up excess moisture. Draw a simple design on the flat surface and then cut around it with a sharp knife. Partially cut parallel to the surface, removing the non-design sections of potato.

3 Before stamping on the cardboard, test the stamp on scrap paper. Brush thick paint onto the stamp and press it firmly onto the paper. If areas of the design do not print, you might need to cut a slice off the raised section. When ready, reapply paint and stamp onto the cardboard.

4 When the paint is dry, glue the cardboard into hat shapes. The pirate hat has a circlet of stiff card inside it so that it fits the head and holds its shape.

PROJECT 36

Sachets

Once you have made the linocut of this floral design, you could also use it to decorate tableware, curtains, and other furnishings.

YOU WILL NEED
cotton fabric
linoleum
a pencil
tracing paper
linoleum cutters
fabric paint
a roller
sewing equipment
ribbon

1 ▶ Trace the design and transfer it onto a piece of linoleum so that the design is reversed (see page 14). Cut along the lines of the design with a straight blade angled away from the stamping areas. Scoop out non-stamping areas with a U-gouge. The dots are cut by twisting a U-gouge vertically.

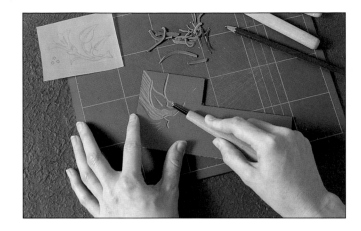

2 ▲ Cut a 9 " square of cotton fabric. Fold it in half, crease the fold and open it out again. Apply fabric paint to the linocut with a roller. Test the linocut by pressing it on scrap paper and recut any areas which do not print sharply. Reapply paint and stamp the fabric in the position shown.

3 ◀ Staystitch the edges of the fabric to prevent fraying. Sew a ½ " seam along the top edge. Fold the fabric along the crease, right sides facing, and sew a ¼ " seam along the side and base.

4 ▶ Turn the sachet right side out and turn in the top edge by 2 ". Fill the sachet with lavender or potpourri and tie a ribbon tightly around the neck.

Monoprinting

The last chapter touched on the use of stamping to create repeat patterns. This one covers another form of printing, one where the results are onetime works of art. It is even easier than stamping but, perhaps because it is less constrained and demands some spontaneity, we tend to find it more daunting.

To make a monoprint, an image is made on a flat surface with paint or ink and then paper or fabric is pressed against it to make a print. Only a single print is possible; when the master is reinked, the next print will be slightly different.

This is a technique which offers lots of room for experimentation. The master can be made on glass, acetate, or even a baking tray. Make sure the surface is free of dust and quite flat. The paint can be a thick glaze based on wallpaper-paste, or a purpose-bought

printing ink. There are even water-based paints formulated for printing on fabrics. Whatever the paint type, it should be slow-drying, allowing you time to work your design. The consistency should be quite thick so that it holds a pattern incised in it. For beginners, it is easier to print onto paper, which should be both strong and flexible. If using fabric, choose one composed of natural fibers and wash it well to remove any size.

The greatest freedom lies in the way you apply the paint. You can lay down a thin layer of paint with a roller and then scratch and scrape marks in it (see pages 72-3) or you can lay down your paints with a brush. The latter may seem no different from traditional painting, but there are vital differences for those lacking confidence as an artist. Working on glass or acetate, you can paint over a sketched design and you can easily modify your work before you make it permanent.

A roller is essential for laying down paint smoothly.

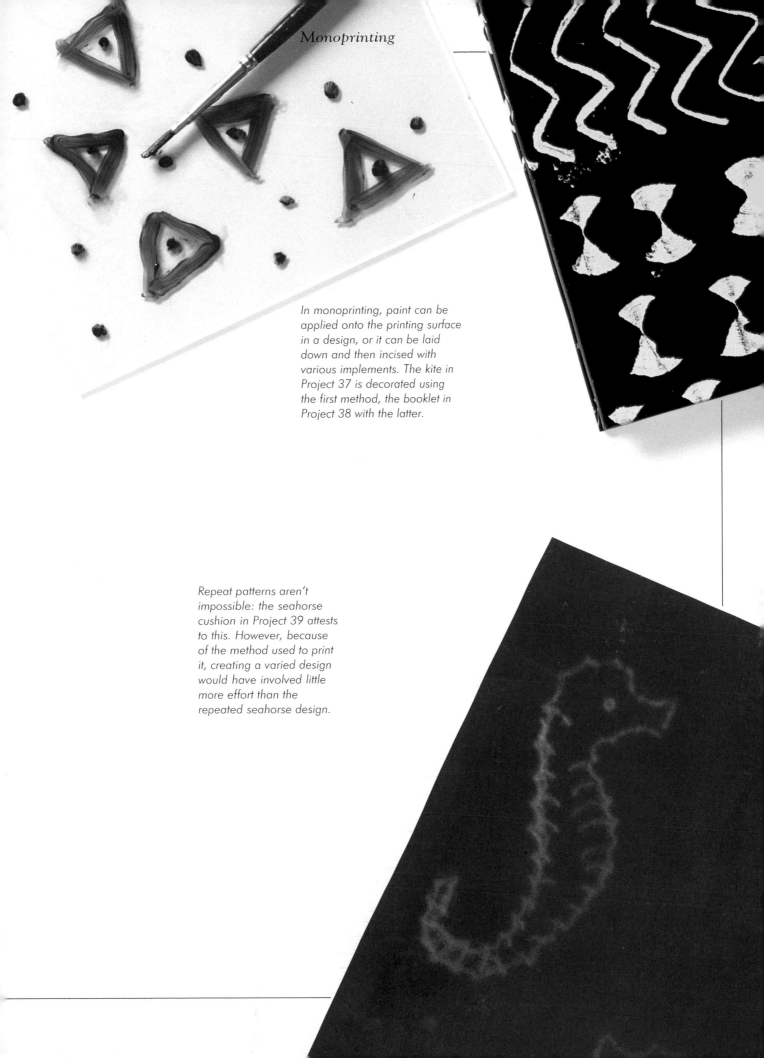

Monoprinting

In monoprinting, paint can be
applied onto the printing surface
in a design, or it can be laid
down and then incised with
various implements. The kite in
Project 37 is decorated using
the first method, the booklet in
Project 38 with the latter.

Repeat patterns aren't
impossible: the seahorse
cushion in Project 39 attests
to this. However, because
of the method used to print
it, creating a varied design
would have involved little
more effort than the
repeated seahorse design.

PROJECT 37

String Kite

String printing is fun for children and adults alike, so you might make this a family activity. Everyone will certainly enjoy flying the finished project.

YOU WILL NEED
strong paper
black paint
string
dowel
a tape measure
glue
a fretsaw
scissors
a curtain ring

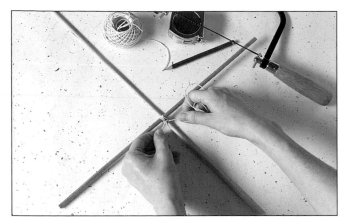

1 Cut two lengths of ¼ " dowel: one 24 " and the other 16 ". Lay the shorter one sideways, a third of the way down the longer one, forming a cross. Bind them tightly at the center with string.

2 With a fretsaw, notch each end of the dowels so that the cuts are all at the same angle. Wind a length of string from notch to notch, forming a diamond shape, and tie the two ends of the string together tightly.

3 Cut a 26 x 18 " sheet of strong paper, fold it lengthwise and open it out again. Dip pieces of string in a bowl of black paint. Lay the strings in coils on one side of the fold with the ends at one edge. Fold the paper and lay a large book on top. Carefully pull the strings out, one by one, and then open out the decorated paper.

4 Cut the decorated paper to 1 " larger than the kite frame. Trim the corners to the dowels. Fold the edges over the string and glue them down securely. Fold 22 " of string in half, loop it through a curtain ring, then tie each end to the kite sides. Tie another string to the kite top, thread it through the ring and secure the other end at the base.

5 Cut scraps of printed paper into butterfly shapes approximately 6 " wide. Gather each piece in the center and tie eight or so onto a length of string at 10 " intervals. Tie the tail onto the base of the kite frame. Attach a flying string to the curtain ring.

PROJECT 38

Concertina Book

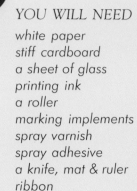

Monoprints are, by definition, unique works of art so they make suitable cover panels for this very personal notebook.

YOU WILL NEED

white paper
stiff cardboard
a sheet of glass
printing ink
a roller
marking implements
spray varnish
spray adhesive
a knife, mat & ruler
ribbon

1 Clean a piece of glass at least 6 " square in size. Lay some printing ink thickly on the glass and spread it evenly with a roller or a flat brush. Using a variety of household items, mark patterns in the paint. If you don't like the design, re-roll the paint and start again.

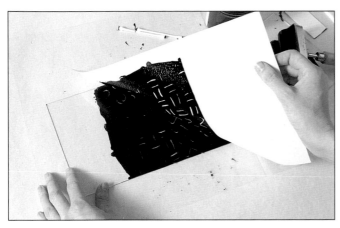

2 Lay a sheet of white paper over the paint. Smooth over the paper with a clean roller or with the heel of your hand. Peel the paper off carefully. Repeat the process with a fresh sheet of paper.

3 Cut two 5½ " squares of cardboard. When the monoprints are dry, spray the back of each with adhesive and glue onto a cardboard square. Miter the paper at the corners, turn the edges over and glue them down neatly. Spray the front of both panels with varnish.

4 Cut a 5 " strip of strong white paper, at least 30 " long. Make pencil marks at 5 " intervals along the top and base. Fold at these marks, turning the paper strip each time to create a concertina. Add extra "pages" to the notebook by gluing such folded sections together.

5 Lay a covered panel face down. Cut two 16 " lengths of ribbon and glue or tape one at either side of the back panel as shown. Glue the back of the concertina pages onto the back panel and then glue the front panel on top.

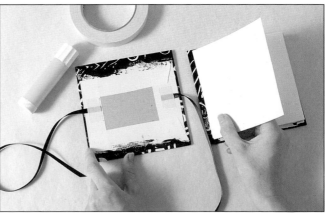

PROJECT 39

Seahorse Cushion

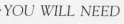

YOU WILL NEED

linen or cotton
acetate or glass
fabric paint
a roller
a pencil & paper
tracing paper
bias binding
piping cord
cushion filling
sewing equipment

It's easy to add your own variations – shells, starfish, seaweed – to this cushion, as this method allows you to sketch out the design before printing.

1 ▶ Cut a piece of white paper the size you wish to make your cushion. Trace the seahorse pattern and transfer it onto the paper by flipping the tracing paper and penciling over the lines on the back. To reverse the design, simply flip the tracing paper again.

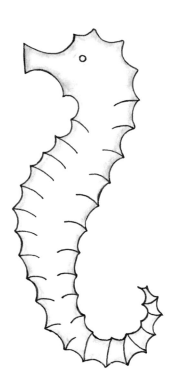

2 ◀ Cut two pieces of a natural fabric, such as linen or cotton, to the desired size. On a large piece of acetate or glass, roll out a very thin layer of fabric paint. Gently lay a piece of fabric down onto the paint.

3 ◀ Lay the design face up on the fabric and tape it in place. Run an implement such as a pencil or knitting needle over the lines of the design, taking care not to press too much on other areas while working. Lift the paper and peel off the fabric, then leave it to dry. Fix the paint as per the instructions.

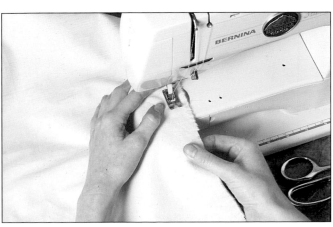

4 ◀ Encase piping cord in a length of colored bias binding and tack this around the printed design so that the edges of the fabric and the binding are aligned. Lay the back section on top and sew around the edges, allowing a generous seam and sewing as close to the cording as possible. Give careful attention to where the cording meets and leave a gap unsewn for turning.

Trim the corners at an angle. Turn the cushion right side out. Fill it with plenty of stuffing and handsew the opening closed.

Stenciling

Stenciling is based on the idea of masking off areas so that paint reaches the surface selectively, in this case in a design which has been cut in a strong material. It is a good way of painting repeat patterns as a stencil can be reused indefinitely. Ready-cut stencils can be bought but it is very easy to cut your own.

A stencil design must have "bridges" built into it to hold the stencil together: some images will need to be simplified or stylized to suit this painting technique. Stencils can be cut from clear acetate, which allows you to see the pattern beneath when cutting and is easy to position on the surface for painting. Acetate can be difficult to cut without slipping so you may prefer to use plain, thin cardboard. You will need to transfer the design (see page 14) onto the card before cutting and you should apply a coat of sealer once it has been cut, as this will extend its life.

Cut the design with a sharp craft knife, taking care not to slip and cut into the masked area. You can use masking tape to hold the cut stencil in position and to ensure that it lies flat against the painting surface.

Stencil brushes have short, stiff bristles of an even length and are used in a downward, dabbing motion. The consistency of the paint must be reasonably thick; if it is too thin, it will seep under the edges of the stencil and blur the design. Dab excess paint onto scrap paper before working on the actual surface. Work inwards from the edges of the design. For large areas, you could stencil with a sponge, giving a softer, broken finish. After removing the stencil, wipe it clean for reuse.

If you wish to paint a design in two or more colors, you can use the one stencil and mask off some areas, or you can cut separate stencils for each color and apply them in stages. If you use this second method, make sure you position each stencil carefully or the colors will be out of alignment.

To cut your own stencils, you will need a sharp craft knife and, ideally, a cutting mat. A stencil brush is the only unusual piece of equipment required; choose a size to suit your project.

Stencils are ideal for repeat
patterns, as in a wall frieze,
or for decorating sets of
things, such as stationery,
menu scrolls, matching
games, or bookplates.

Keep your stencil designs
simple and remember to
include enough bridges
to hold the cut stencil
together. Other designs
in this book, such as
the flower in Project 36,
can be modified for
stenciling.

PROJECT 40

Writing Paper

Notepaper decorated with a simple stencil is a delight to write on. A bundle of such paper with matching envelopes also makes a charming gift.

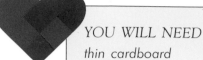

YOU WILL NEED
thin cardboard
writing paper
envelopes
tracing paper
a pencil
a knife & mat
water-based varnish
water-based paints
a stencil brush

1 ▶ Cut a piece of thin cardboard the same width as your writing paper. Transfer the design onto this (see page 14) and cut along the lines carefully with a sharp knife. Apply a coat of water-based varnish to both sides of the stencil so that it lasts longer.

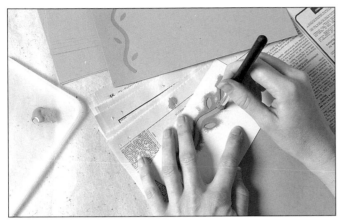

2 ◀ Lay the stencil along the top of a sheet of writing paper and hold it in place. Load a stencil brush with water-based paint and dab any excess on scrap paper. Apply paint with a stippling action, making sure that no paint seeps under the stencil. Lift the stencil off carefully.

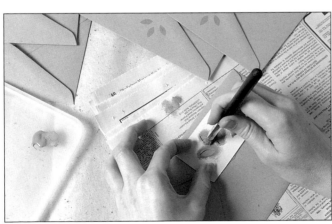

3 ◀ Use the smaller design to stencil a motif on the flap of each envelope. Use colors that contrast with the background so that the design shows up clearly.

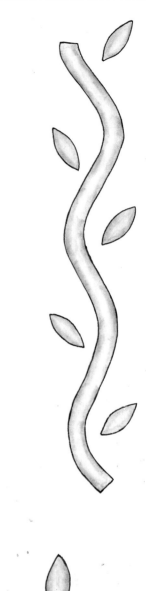

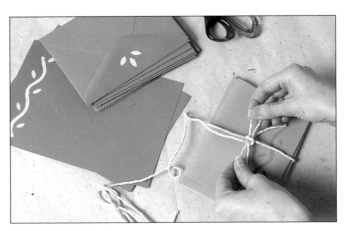

4 ◀ Fold the sheets of writing paper in half, with the design visible on top. Tie sheets and envelopes into bundles with string or matching ribbon.

PROJECT 41

Table Linen

This African design makes a striking set of tablemats and napkins. It is stenciled in two stages, working one color and then the next.

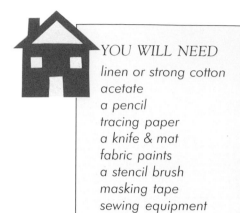

1 Cut suitable fabric, such as linen or strong cotton, into large rectangles for placemats and squares for napkins. Turn over ¼ " at each edge and iron the fold. Trim the corners at an angle. Turn over another ¼ " and machine sew the hem, giving special attention to the corners.

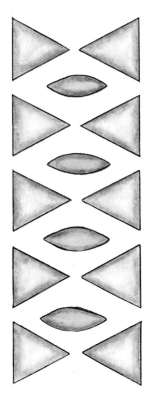

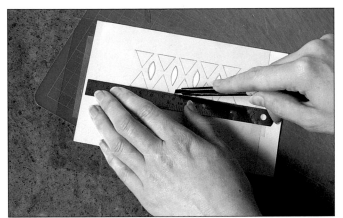

2 Trace the design onto paper. Lay the tracing on a cutting mat and tape a piece of clear acetate over it. Use a ruler and a sharp knife to cut out the colored areas of the design, taking great care not to slip.

3 Cover the black areas of the design with pieces of masking tape. Position the stencil along one edge of the placemat as shown. Dip the stencil brush in brown fabric paint and dab the excess on scrap paper. Stencil the unmasked sections of the design, moving the stencil when necessary. Paint all the linen with this color first.

4 Remove the masking tape and mask the brown design areas of the stencil. When the brown paint is dry, align the acetate over it and stencil the black sections. Once the paint is dry, fix it according to the manufacturer's instructions.

PROJECT 42

Letter Blocks

Wooden blocks are an enduring toy for each generation of children to enjoy. Make sure you use non-toxic paints and varnish to decorate them.

YOU WILL NEED
timber
a saw
sandpaper
a ruler & pencil
tracing paper
acetate or cardboard
a knife & mat
water-based paints
a stencil brush
water-based varnish

1 ▶ You will need a length of timber 1½ x 1½ ". Mark and cut twelve sections, each 1½ " long, to create twelve cubes. Smooth the edges and corners with fine sandpaper.

2 ◀ Paint each of the blocks with several coats of water-based paint. You can paint each in a single color, or in different colors on each face, which requires a bit more care.

3 ▶ Trace the letters on page 158. Cut twenty-six squares of acetate. Position an acetate square over a letter and carefully cut along the lines with a sharp knife to remove the letter shape. If you are making cardboard stencils, transfer the letter onto the card and then cut it out.

4 ◀ Position a letter stencil on one face of a block and dab cream-colored paint through the stencil, using a stiff brush. Stencil different letters on each block face, working your way through the alphabet, so that each letter appears at least once. When dry, apply a coat of non-toxic varnish.

Gilt Touches

For thousands of years, gilding has been used to imply that an object is made of solid gold; as such it is one of the earliest false finishes. Traditionally, this illusion was achieved by gluing a thin sheet of gold or gold-colored metal onto a surface and this is still a wonderful way to gild large areas. Today, however, excellent gold paints are available which allow you greater freedom in the way you use gold in your creations.

The art of gilding with metal leaf is regaining popularity and is still worked in much the same way as it has been through the centuries. The various materials needed are often available in a kit. The surface must be sealed and prepared carefully: flaws and imperfections will be highlighted once gilded.

A basecoat of bole, a clay-colored pigment, throws up warmth through the thin metal sheets. Size, a liquid glue with a milky consistency, is then applied wherever you wish to gild. Gold leaf is very fragile and must be cut into manageable pieces. These are carefully laid on the sized areas in an overlapping arrangement and then "tamped" or brushed down with a flat brush. A firm brushing with a bristle brush dislodges any overlapping leaf: the flakes left over are known as "skew", which can be used for covering gaps. Products for aging and varnishing can also be applied.

Gold paint, either water-based or solvent-based, is certainly easier to apply and is necessary when creating designs or adding fine lines. Some paint ranges offer a selection of golds from pale to rich. Do not thin gold paint too much or the result will be dull. While it may be tempting to be lavish, a little gold goes a long way. A fine spatter, a thin trim, or a delicate smear of gold can lift a project dramatically without overpowering it.

A covering of gold leaf or Dutch gold can suggest that an object is made of solid gold. Detail, on the other hand, must be worked in gold paint.

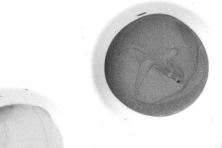

Found objects from the natural world can become treasures when given the gold treatment. Difficult shapes, such as cones and seedpods, are most easily covered with spray paint.

Gold wax, available in tubes or jars, can be rubbed onto a surface with your fingertip. It is particularly effective on objects with details in relief.

PROJECT 43

Leaf Jewelry

The most imaginative jewelry can be made with
inexpensive materials, and a mere hint of gold paint
will ensure these pieces catch every eye.

YOU WILL NEED
plywood
tracing paper
a pencil
a saw
sandpaper
water-based paints
painting equipment
varnish
jewelry fittings
strong glue

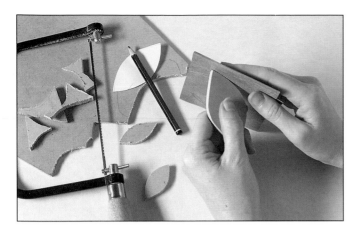

1 Trace the patterns and then transfer them onto plywood. Use a fretsaw or a jigsaw to cut out one large leaf and two smaller leaves. Smooth the edges of each piece with sandpaper.

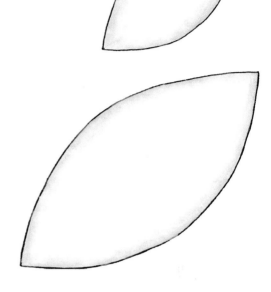

2 Basecoat each piece with turquoise paint, applying a second or third coat if necessary. When the base-coat is dry, paint the leaf veins in gold paint, using a liner brush.

3 When the veins are dry, thin some gold paint with a litle water and wipe it around the edges of each leaf with your fingertip. Be careful not to apply the paint too heavily. Once the paint is dry, apply a coat of varnish to each piece.

4 Check the best position for the jewelry fittings. Use a strong glue to attach a brooch clasp to the back of the large leaf, and an earring clip to each of the smaller leaves.

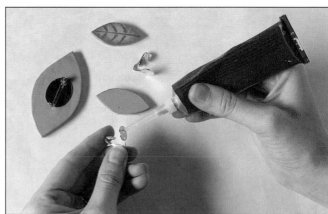

PROJECT 44

Chessboard

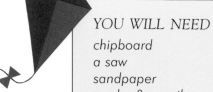

This beautiful chessboard will bring out the very best in your game. It is gilded with Dutch gold – imitation gold leaf which is an alloy of zinc and copper.

YOU WILL NEED
chipboard
a saw
sandpaper
a ruler & pencil
bole
size
gold leaf
black paint
gold leaf varnish
painting equipment

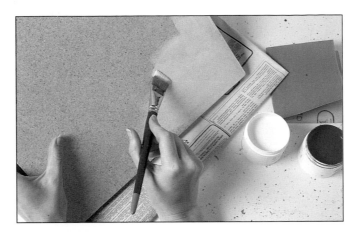

1 ◀ Cut a 13½ " square of chipboard at least ½ " thick. Sand the edges and surfaces well until smooth. Apply a coat of white water-based undercoat. Apply at least two coats of bole (red clay primer).

2 ▲ Measure and mark a grid of eight by eight squares, each 1½ ", with a ¾ " border around the edge. Start at a corner and paint size (an adhesive liquid) onto every second square in a row.

3 ▲ Carefully cut 1 " squares of gold leaf. Test the size after five or six minutes: it should be tacky to touch. Lower the gold leaf onto a sized square and smooth it down with a dry brush. Lay other pieces so that they overlap slightly and exceed the boundaries of the sized squares.

4 ▶ Repeat the last step until every second square and all the border is gilded. Brush gently but firmly over the gold leaf with a bristle brush. This will dislodge any excess gold leaf. Save these flakes, which are known as "skew."

5 ▶ Paint the ungilded squares in black. Apply dots of size and sprinkle the skew over them so that the black squares are speckled with gold. Brush off any loose skew and brush over the board with a bristle brush. Apply a coat of gold leaf varnish over the whole board.

PROJECT 45

Gilt Clock

Clay-red and gold are a classic combination of tones. Clock mechanisms are available from some craft stores or you can dismantle an inexpensive clock.

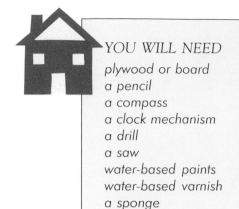

YOU WILL NEED
plywood or board
a pencil
a compass
a clock mechanism
a drill
a saw
water-based paints
water-based varnish
a sponge
painting equipment

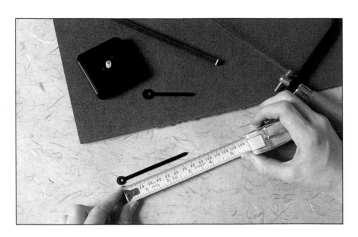

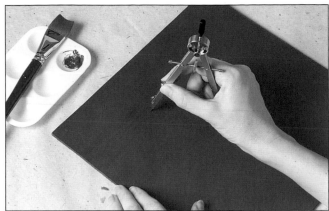

1 Cut a square piece of stiff board, 1½ " wider than the longest hand of your clock mechanism. The clock in the picture measures 8½ " square.

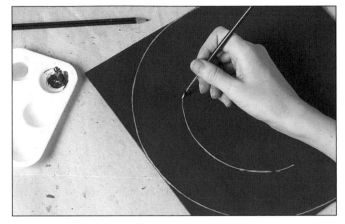

2 Apply two coats of clay-red paint. Locate and mark the center of the square. Use a compass to draw a circle just within the square and another circle 2 " in from that.

3 Paint over the pencil rings in gold with a fine liner brush. With a pencil, mark twelve dots evenly around the ring. Over these, draw the Roman numerals (or trace and transfer them from page 156). Paint each numeral in gold.

4 Once the paint has dried, cover the circle with scrap paper. Load gold paint onto a sponge and wipe over each corner. Paint the hands of the clock mechanism gold.

5 In the center, drill a hole large enough to fit the spindle of the clock. Varnish the face of the board. Assemble the clock and tape the mechanism to the back of the board.

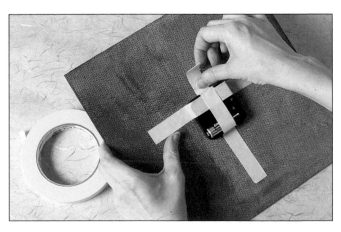

False Finishes

For almost as long as certain materials have been prized, artisans have been creating techniques to mimic them. This was not always merely a cost-saving exercise. When building a palace, marble might be too heavy to use for ceilings, whereas a painted finish could produce the same effect on a lighter material. Generally, though, it was because the material was rare and expensive. Some, like tortoiseshell, we would not choose to use these days but we can still appreciate their appearance.

Using relatively simple ingredients, techniques were developed to apply expensive woodgrains to cheap timber, to simulate rare lacquerware from the East, even to paint architectural details in a *trompe l'oeil*, literally, a trick of the eye.

With modern paints and mediums, these techniques are now easier to achieve. They still require some patience but the basics have already been covered in the earlier chapters on sponging, spattering, and ragging.

Today, what are collectively known as "faux finishes" have regained popularity and are fashionable techniques in home decorating. For some of us, though, a whole room of paint effect can be a little overwhelming, both to attempt and to live in. There are plenty of small projects which are more manageable and still make a dramatic impact.

Boxes, or flat mats, such as the coasters in Project 27, are ideal for beginners. Frames, planters, and small items of furniture are just some of the other possibilities. Project 47 takes false finishes into another dimension, showing how to turn plain cardboard into antique metal relief. Not quite base metal into gold – but near enough!

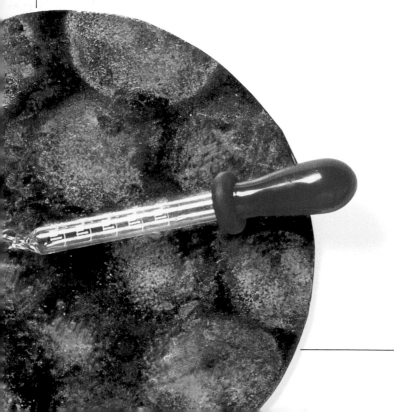

Tortoiseshell
Basecoat the surface black and, when dry, seal it. With a damp sponge, randomly apply patches of pale gold, rich gold, and bronze, covering the entire surface. Thin black paint to the consistency of milk and paint a small area with this wash. While it is wet, apply droplets of isopropyl alcohol with an eyedropper. The black paint will disperse, revealing the paint below. Treat the entire surface in this way.

Lapis lazuli
Basecoat the surface sapphire blue. Sponge on ultramarine blue to cover a third of the surface. Allowing each color to dry before applying the next, sponge on sparing amounts of teal green and pale gold. Apply these in drifts across the surface. When dry, apply a coat of varnish.

Green marble
Basecoat the surface black. Apply a green glaze in wriggles with a round brush, by laying the brush on its side and twisting it across the surface until it is three-quarters covered. While this is still wet, rag it by pressing it with crumpled newspaper.

Apply the major veins in thinned white paint with a medium-sized pointed brush or the tip of a feather. Hold it loosely and draw it towards you, twisting it to produce uneven, broken lines. Dab the lines with a large bristle brush to soften. With a fine pointed brush, draw a web of white secondary veins. These should be finer and more spidery than the major veins. When dry, varnish to bring out the colors.

PROJECT 46

Lacquer Frame

YOU WILL NEED
a wooden frame
black paint
red paint
painting equipment
wet-&-dry paper
a sponge or cloth
gloss varnish

Real Japanese lacquer is a rare substance made from tree sap. Western furniture-makers have been trying to imitate its richness in paint and varnish for centuries.

1 ▶ If you are using an old frame, sand it back until the surface is smooth. Apply an even coat of black paint and allow it to dry. Repeat until the timber is not visible through the paint.

2 ▶ Apply a coat of red paint over the black. When it is dry, sand it lightly and then apply further coats of red until the basecoat is covered. The topcoat should be very smooth, without noticeable brushstrokes, so thin the paint if necessary.

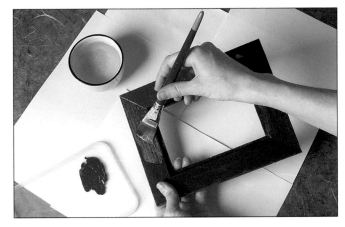

3 ▶ When the topcoat is dry, wet a piece of wet-&-dry paper and lightly rub sections of the frame. Wipe it regularly with a sponge or cloth so you can see the effect. Distress the paintwork until a hint of black paint appears through the red.

4 ▶ Wipe the frame with a lint-free cloth to remove any dust. Apply a coat of gloss polyurethane varnish and allow it to dry. Apply four or five more coats of varnish, sanding between coats and leaving the frame to dry in a dust-free place.

PROJECT 47

Money Box

This wonderful treasure chest can be made from an old box or constructed afresh from pieces of strong cardboard, as shown here.

YOU WILL NEED
strong cardboard
a ruler & pencil
a knife & mat
white glue
a glue gun
water-based paints
water-based varnish
painting equipment
dark shoe polish
a cloth

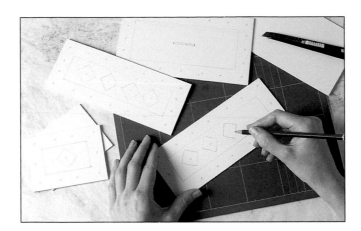

1 ◄ Measure and cut the box sections from cardboard. The box shown has: two 7½ x 3 " sides; two 4 x 3 " ends, an 7¼ x 4 " base and matching top. On one side of each section, draw a pattern of dots and diamonds. Cut a slot for money in the lid.

2 ▲ Lay the relief design with a tube of white glue or with very thick white paint in an icing nozzle. Allow the relief work to set; this may take a couple of days. Use a hot glue gun or other strong adhesive to glue the sections of the box together.

3 ▲ Apply a coat of bright blue acrylic paint on all sides of the box. This enhances the silver topcoat.

4 ◄ Paint the box with silver acrylic paint, applying a second or third coat if necessary.

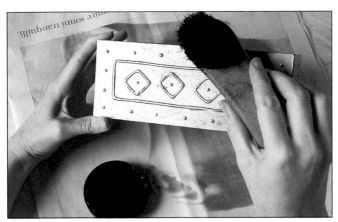

5 ◄ Apply some dark shoe polish over the relief work and wipe off the excess with a rag. Varnish the box to complete.

PROJECT 48

Marbled Case

With patience, you can use paint to mimic marbled stone, such as Sienna marble. Slow drying oil paints produce even more realistic effects than the acrylics used here.

1 Undercoat the box. Mix a touch of raw sienna with white paint and basecoat the box evenly. Lay patches of burnt sienna, raw sienna and vermilion glazes (for more on glazes, see page 12).

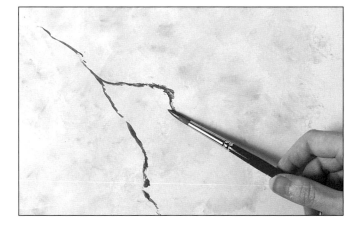

2 While the glaze patches are still wet, blot the surface with a lint-free cloth to smudge them. Dab with a large dry brush to soften the edges, cleaning the brush constantly on a rag.

3 Apply the major veins with a medium-sized pointed brush. Load the brush with blue-black paint. Hold it loosely and draw it towards you, twisting it to produce uneven, broken lines. Again, dab the lines with a large brush to soften.

4 With the pointed brush, apply patches of white along sections of the veins. Soften the edges of these patches, as above.

5 With a fine pointed brush, draw a web of blue-black secondary veins. These should be finer and more spidery than the major veins. When dry, varnish the box and attach the clasp and hinges.

Instant Age

There are many projects for which a clean, bright finish is just what you require. On other occasions you may want to give a newly painted item a patina of age, softening the colors, making an article appear well-handled and much-loved. This can be useful when decorating a room with a mixture of old and new furniture.

There are various antiquing techniques. One of the most popular is distressing: rubbing the topcoat to reveal the wood grain or basecoat underneath. To distress a piece, rub the paintwork along the grain with wet-and-dry paper dipped in soapy water. Wipe with a cloth regularly to check on progress.

A glaze of paint in an earthy tone can be rubbed into the surface of paintwork to suggest the grime of passing years. Such colors as raw umber, burnt umber, and burnt sienna are ideal for this form of antiquing which appears in Project 51.

Some finishes are designed to imitate processes used in times past, indicating age by implication. One of these is "sugi", described below. A related one is liming, in which white emulsion is applied to raw timber and partially removed to mimic the lime treatment once used to prevent worm infestation. Like sugi, liming produces a soft effect which highlights the grain of inexpensive timber.

Some metals age in an unusual manner: copper, brass and bronze can turn a chalky blue-green through long exposure to air. This effect, known by the French as *vert de Grece* (the green of Greece), is today called "verdigris" and is a popular decorative finish. Project 50 shows how to simulate it with paint, allowing you to apply a verdigris finish to surfaces other than metal.

All antiquing should be subtle. Consider which area of an item would receive the most wear – the edges of a box, the seat of a chair, the handles on a chest of drawers – or where dirt would most likely collect. Give those areas special attention and your project will look as though it has grown old gracefully.

During the 15th century, Eastern craftspeople used a flame to give wood a lightly charred finish, known as "sugi". This aging effect can be imitated by coating black-painted timber with surface filler. Once the filler has dried, sand it in the direction of the grain, wipe with a damp cloth, and apply a coat of varnish.

Distressing

Once dry, paintwork can be rubbed lightly with wet-and-dry paper which has been dipped in soapy water. If the piece is to be decorated with a delicate design, distress the base color first, then paint the design and give it a light sanding to finish.

Crackling

Paint often cracks as it ages and this effect can be simulated instantly by applying a crackle medium between the basecoat and topcoat. Fine cracks in varnish can be achieved by covering a slow-drying oil-based varnish with a quick-drying water-based one.

Glazing

Mix a glaze (see page 12) tinted with an oil paint or an acrylic in an earthy tone. Rub the glaze into the painted surface and then wipe off the excess. The glaze will remain in any cracks and crevices, so this technique is very effective when combined with either of the two above.

PROJECT 49

Crackled Boxes

A brand new set of nested boxes could be mistaken for antiques with the application of crackle medium and a gilt trim.

YOU WILL NEED
a set of boxes
acrylic paints
crackle medium
water-based varnish
painting equipment
a sponge

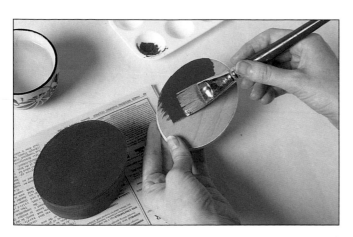

1 ◀ *If repainting old boxes, see page 13 for information on preparation. Basecoat the outside of each box with rust-colored paint, applying a second coat if necessary. Allow to dry.*

2 ◀ *Apply an even coat of crackle medium over the basecoat with a flat brush. Leave the medium to set for the time recommended by the manufacturer, usually twenty minutes to one hour.*

3 ▶ *Apply a topcoat of cream paint with a sponge or with quick brush strokes, painting thickly for large cracks or thinly for fine ones. Do not reapply paint once the crackling process begins.*

4 ▶ *When the topcoat is dry, paint a trim in gold acrylic paint with a fine liner brush. Paint the inside of the boxes if desired. Apply a coat of water-based varnish to protect the crackle work.*

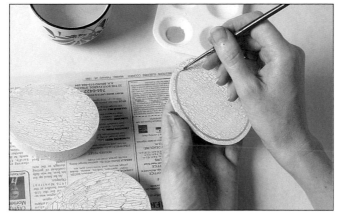

PROJECT 50

Verdigris Planter

YOU WILL NEED
a terracotta planter
sealer
water-based paints
painting equipment
a sponge

An inexpensive planter box can quickly be disguised as aging metal. This one is terracotta and so needs sealing before the paint is applied.

1 ◄ Apply a coat of sealer or water-based varnish to all surfaces of the terracotta planter box. When this is dry, apply a basecoat of dark gray paint. The basecoat should be opaque and even.

2 ▲ Dab a sponge in copper paint and remove the excess on scrap paper. Sponge the paint onto the surface in a light, random pattern.

3 ▲ When the copper paint is dry, sponge on turquoise paint in a similar fashion.

4 ◄ Apply turquoise paint onto a large brush and use your fingers to spatter it onto the surface.

5 ◄ Add a touch of white paint and a few drops of water to the turquoise and spatter this mixture onto the surface. Dab the surface lightly with a sponge to remove excess paint and allow it to dry. Apply a coat of varnish to protect the paintwork.

PROJECT 51

Jumping Jack

*Such toys as these were very popular in Victorian times.
A light tint can give your version the appearance of
belonging to that era.*

YOU WILL NEED

plywood
tracing paper
a pencil
a fretsaw & drill
sandpaper
water-based paints
painting equipment
pliers & small nails
strong thread
a large bead

1 ▲ Trace the toy pattern which can be found on page 159. Cut out paper templates or trace the shapes onto plywood. Use a fretsaw to cut out the plywood pieces. Sand the edges of each piece.

2 ▲ Paint the pieces with water-based paints. Apply the base colors first. When these are dry, mark the facial features and other details in pencil and then paint over them with a very fine liner brush.

3 ▶ Mix some brown paint with a medium to thin the color. Apply this glaze around the edges of each piece to suggest grime from handling. Wipe off any excess paint. Apply a coat of varnish.

4 ▶ Drill small holes where indicated on the pattern; these should be larger than your nails. Tie the two upper leg sections together as shown, with enough thread to allow them to be pinned to the body by the remaining holes. Tie the arm sections together likewise.

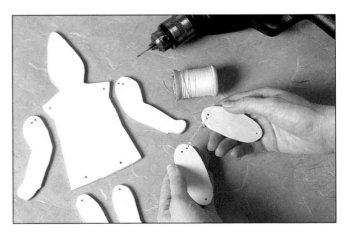

5 ▶ Connect the parts with small nails. Bend the tip of each nail over at the back, so that the limbs can move freely. Attach a long thread to the arm and leg cross-threads so that when pulled down, the limbs move. Knot a large bead at the bottom of the string.

Gift Giving

Having turned your hand to paint crafts and discovered hidden talents, you can now present your masterpieces to friends and family who will no doubt appreciate them almost as much as you do! Many of the projects in this book make wonderful and practical gifts and it is always a pleasure to receive something which has been handmade.

Many of the techniques in this book are ideal for decorating paper to make giftwrap. Buy a large roll of inexpensive unsized paper or recycle brown paper or large paper shopping bags, which can then be stamped, spattered, stenciled, or whatever. When you

are making any of the projects, decorate some paper in the same fashion so you have a ready supply of giftwrap and cards.

For items that are difficult to wrap, boxes and giftbags are a good solution. A touch of paint can give a second lease of life to an old shoebox. Inexpensive papier-mâché boxes are available in all shapes and sizes from craft stores and, once decorated, can be a gift in themselves. Giftbags can be made to fit any present. Decorate the paper first before constructing the bag by following the instructions on page 91. For extra decoration, paint a few trimmings. String can be dipped in paint to match the paper. Spray paint can turn interesting shapes and textures into eye-catching tokens.

From left to right: giftwraps made by resistworks, sponging, scraping, and stamping.

A touch of gold
spray paint turns
everyday items into
beautiful trimmings.

Brown paper with
paint scraped
onto it makes a
striking statement.

This star-stamped
giftbag is easy to
make and ideal for
presents which
don't wrap neatly.

Making Tags & Cards

For those occasions when a greeting card is more appropriate than a gift, paint and paper are invaluable. Whether it be a unique design or mass production of cards at Christmas, you will find a suitable technique involving paint.

To frame a design in a card, use a three-panel mount such as the star card shown on the top right of page 155. Blank mounts can be bought or you can make your own by folding a piece of card into three panels, cutting a window in the center panel, and securing the painted paper or fabric behind it.

Alternatively, decorated paper or fabric can simply be glued on the front of a two-panel card. Scraps of marbling or a simple monoprint can become miniature works of art when presented in this way. Choose strong paper or thin card in a color to suit your paintwork.

The most efficient way to make cards, especially large numbers at one time, is to apply paint directly onto the front of a two panel card. Choose light-colored cardboard on which paint will show up clearly. Then you can either cut and fold the card first, or decorate it and then make up the cards. The design can be on both the front and back, but leave the inside clear for your message!

Gift tags can be cut from scraps and offcuts of other projects. They tend to have a shorter lifespan than cards but can make all the difference to a gift's presentation.

Clockwise:
A two-panel card stamped with an eraser-cut; a three-panel mount framing marbled fabric; a leaf print; oil-on-water marbling; a label gift tag; a small batik card; a stenciled tag.

*Border and boss patterns
for Project 3*

Numerals pattern for Project 45

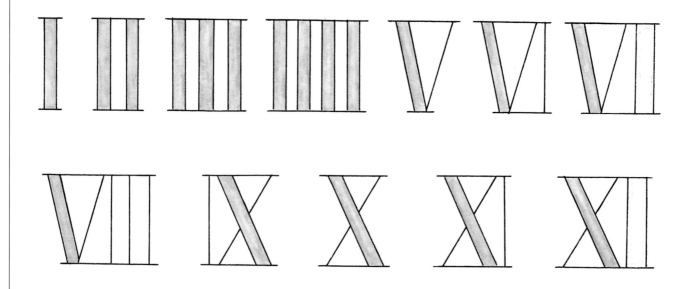

Basic gift bag shape for Project 28

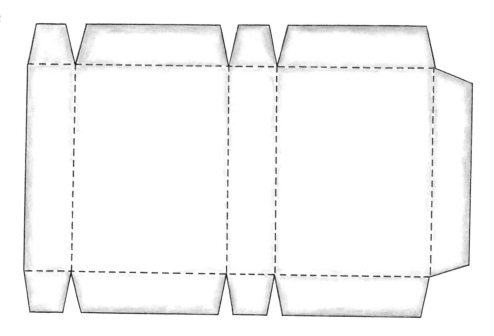

Stained glass pattern for Project 18

Letter pattern for Project 42

ABCDEF
GHIJKL
MNOPQ
RSTUV
WXYZ

Jumping Jack pattern for Project 51

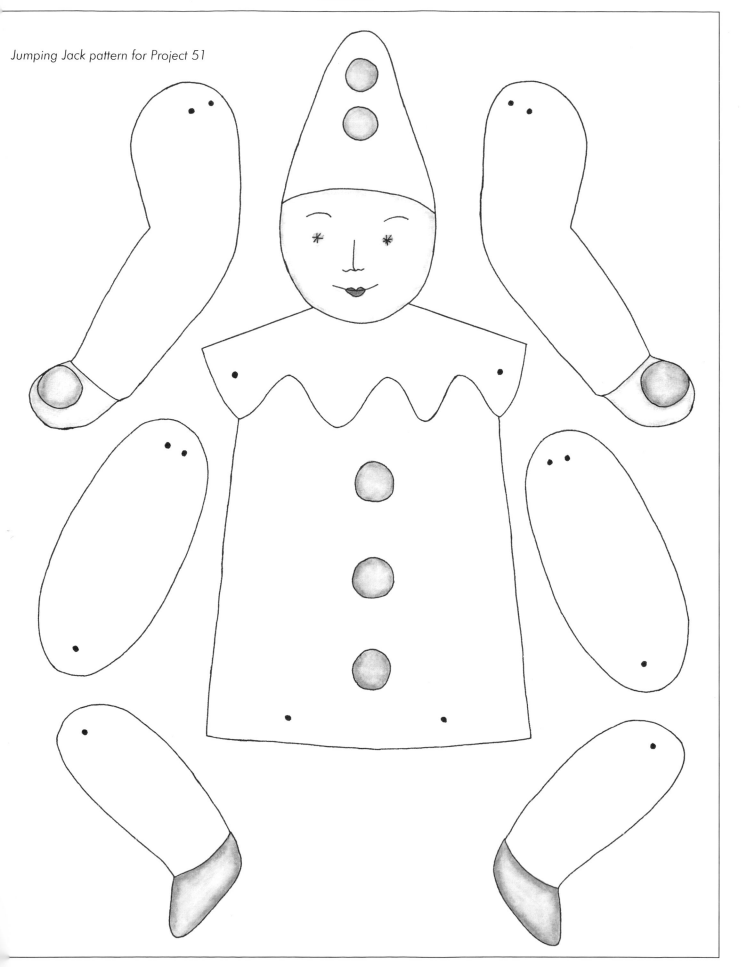

Index